KABUKI OTHELLO

by
KAREN SUNDE

Conceived by
Shozo Sato

Dramatic Publishing
Woodstock, Illinois • England • Australia • New Zealand

*** NOTICE ***

IMPORTANT BILLING AND CREDIT REQUIREMENTS

PRODUCTION

The stage directions describe a version of Kabuki, but with new elements, e.g., Koken that speak. Companies may use the directions as guide, altering elements to suit their needs and imagination.

Open stage or proscenium with curtain (lightweight). A forestage is useful, and even arena is possible. Moveable set elements—long fabric panels that drop; a screen; a platform for reclining or levels. Whatever is needed, the black-dressed, scurrying Koken arrange it, like invisible elves.

The melody for the song on pages 73-74 can be found at at the back of the book (page 88).

PRODUCTION HISTORY

As *Kabuki Othello*, this play was commissioned and originally produced by the Annenberg Center, University of Pennsylvania; The People's Light & Theatre Company; and Wisdom Bridge Theatre in 1986-87, and also produced at Milwaukee Repertory Theatre and Krannert Center, University of Illinois, and as *Othello's Passion* at Illinois State University in 2006.

KABUKI OTHELLO

A Play in Two Acts

CHARACTERS

EMILIA: Narrator, wife to Iago, lady in waiting to Desdemona.

OTHELLO: The Ainu; heroic general, caveman to the Japanese.

IAGO: High-ranking officer, husband to Emilia, serves Othello.

CASSIO: High-ranking officer, privileged playboy.

DESDEMONA: Brave young noblewoman, wife to Othello.

KOKEN: (4 to 8) Chorus, storytellers who facilitate the action.

KI-PLAYER: Koken who signals the opening of scenes and key moments by striking the "KI" (key) or resounding wooden blocks.

TALKING THE TALK

Making sense of words free in space: Whether one person or several speak a line, the text is meant to flow like ordinary conversation. Lines starting with a small letter mean the previous sentence is still going on. Lines starting with a capital letter mean a new sentence begins here. Ends of lines could mean a comma, semi-colon, a period, or none. There are exceptions, but as in life, the more fun you have with it, the better it works.

ACT ONE

Scene 1

(Flute. KI-Player kneels at edge of stage, strikes KI to open curtain, and to begin performance. Salty, wise EMILIA enters, moves into place, nods to audience, begins to tell them her story—)

EMILIA
It happened in a time
such things could happen
not so very long ago

There came to us
out of the north
up from the earth
an Ainu

In our time of troubles
when even night could not sleep
came an Ainu
to lead us ·

Skin of pale pink
bristled over with hair
a man-beast, an Ainu
we called him Othello

7

(OTHELLO strides on, bold, into spotlight, "mounts" [mimes riding horseback].)

OTHELLO
My horses thunder down hillsides
blades scream in thick air
fire is thrown
against the bitter wind—
these are the life of Othello
Harsh days that
man asks of man
these are mine

(OTHELLO steps aside, strikes Mie (mee-ay) pose, as IAGO scurries on into spotlight.)

IAGO
Iago, I am
Mine is to serve
what man asks of man
brain and back
arm and eye
no task too hard
no time too long
I serve him, Othello, the Ainu
I am Iago

(IAGO strikes Mie pose by OTHELLO, as CASSIO enters preening into spotlight.)

CASSIO
Cassio is me
Othello is the man
I'd like to be
His life is cut exact and swift
an arrow leaping
from a spring of steel
while Cassio can only reel
straying off the target
into meadows deep with flowers

(CASSIO strikes Mie pose, making a tableau with OTHELLO and IAGO. Then DESDEMONA glides in softly, as EMILIA narrates.)

EMILIA
Silent as a waiting child
her step as gentle
deer step
she comes among them
parting waves of man air
she comes fearless
Desdemona

(The focus of all three men is drawn to DESDEMONA, who stands apart. OTHELLO nears her first. At each stop of the wheel, one man speaks his inner desires, aside, to audience—)

OTHELLO
In my fist
she'd be a fragile bird

no bold leg, no ready laugh
like women of the camp

Why does she gaze at me
She'd smash between one finger
and my thumb
My hairy face, round Ainu eyes
should frighten her
She should look away

Shall I answer her?

IAGO
Desdemona is a word
I whisper
only deep at night
That word alone is blessing
my coarse tongue
can touch it only
secretly
Desdemona

CASSIO
Each woman enchants me
rhyming breath in my ear
brilliant silk on my skin
"Cassio" they say "won't be long
selecting this night's lady"

> (*RONDO DANCE: Circle of three men dance, gradually
> increasing their tempo, while EMILIA prepares us for
> her prediction—*)

EMILIA
What sways the willow
over quiet water
what whisper of pink sky
swells the bud

What stirs
and once it stirs
will happen?

(OTHELLO carried away with his passion—)

OTHELLO
Desdemona
Her voice sweeps my temples
bright as dawn rain
When I speak
my life shines
in her face
She's mine
I will have her
no power that lives
can damp such a light
once it flows

EMILIA
Life sways the willow
over quiet water
its whisper of pink sky
swells the bud

Life stirs

and once it stirs
will happen

*(KI strikes, and all dancers stop at once, striking a Mie
pose. KI strikes. Curtain closes or KI strikes fast as they
exit.*

*KOKEN enter swiftly, presenting their Choral Ode.
[Make the best distribution of lines for your KOKEN.
Numbers indicate a possible distribution of lines when
there are four KOKEN—"A" indicates that ALL speak
together.] Clear flowing meaning is the goal. Rhythm is
sharp, tight and swift, like one voice speaking naturally,
or like an eager conversation, its excitement heightened
by the group.)*

KOKEN
(1)   Man-time marches
        straight on his line
        never
        marking the wheel

        But let him once
        wait and listen
(3)   In the twilight
        he'll hear
        his younger self
        bark at his heel

(2)   Life
        spins on in cycles

(4)   Woman follows the moon
        marks on her womb
        that time is no line
        but a wheel

(1)   Wind (A) wind on the wheel
(1)   it gathers
        the paths of our lives
        beginning to end
(A)   and back again
(1)   to beginning
(A)   we all arrive

(1)   Cassio
(4)   Desdemona
(2)   Iago
(3)   Othello
(2)   Why do these
        four roll together
        belonging no more
        to each other
        than pebbles
        tossed on the sand
(3)   yet once they have touched
        they will hold
        and each be the fate
        of the other
(1)   sure as clay molded
        in only one hand

(1)   Wind (A) wind on the wheel

(4)   never think
      your dance is your own
(A)   wondering
(3)   why this way (2) why that
(4)   why these cares (1) these desires
(2)   dance in grace
      there is nothing to find
(A)   more than your place
      on the winding wheel

*(KOKEN scurry away as curtain opens or the new scene
is revealed. KI strikes.)*

Scene 2

*(Bright colored silky panels hang the height of the stage.
Each character stands behind the panel that is his color,
then shakes it, in a manner that announces his mood the
instant before he steps out to tell the audience his story.
EMILIA is first to flutter her banner, then step out to
speak—)*

EMILIA
Men stretch their banners
bold against the sky
declare their might
and leave the earth all trembling

We women watch the show
and smile our secret smile
remembering

Emilia, I am
I chose Iago the soldier
more clever than most
not so loud
I couldn't outguess him
and that kept life lively
and Iago my man
served the Ainu

*(OTHELLO's banner shakes boldly, and OTHELLO
steps forth, and dance-tells his battle story.)*

OTHELLO
I, Othello the Ainu
barbaric, untamed
Before me
the smooth skin polite ones
revile us
regard us
only as slaves
take our land
push us back into caves

But on me
they learn to smile
me they praise
in their homes
me raise over their heads
I have amazed them

Invaders from the far seas came
and bled them

chased them
into one small cave
Invaders loomed
across the field between
I ordered "wait"
They strained to fight
but I said "wait"
until they're close enough
to squeeze

I held us still
Invaders thundered in
When I said "now"
our arrows had an easy mark
Then we burst forth
a many-headed serpent
now awaked from sleep
When my arm dropped
they say a hundred dead
spread at my feet
So much blood drenched me
that I was to them
a sight from hell
My name alone
now starts a wave of fear

EMILIA
Yes. He bled the enemy
when we had lost hope
but we honor him too far
that's not wise
He's learned our manners

can mimic our speech
but what smothered growls
lie inside

*(But CASSIO's banner waves gaily before CASSIO steps
out to argue with EMILIA.)*

CASSIO
I know the chambers
of the most refined
Among them all
there is not one
with half
his elegance of heart

EMILIA
Elegance is it
that you're his Lieutenant?

CASSIO
I—Lieutenant?

EMILIA
You did not know
Othello has appointed you?

*(IAGO's banner shakes angrily, and IAGO steps for-
ward, stifling his fury. Simultaneously, CASSIO strikes a
pose of astonished obedience.)*

IAGO
I have my place through loyal service
and loyally I'll keep it

CASSIO
My lord Othello
is greatness
flung among us
I serve
with head inclined
most honored

EMILIA
Greatness? Perhaps
but no one wise
promotes a wanton playboy
to his side

IAGO
Hold your tongue!
Bite down and bear it
The General Othello is truly great
his lieutenant Cassio...must be followed too
his bride—the matchless Desdemona
honors him
and so will we

EMILIA
And something more?
You do not speak your heart
My husband is well trained to serve

but something more is there
Can great Othello read it?

*(DESDEMONA's banner flutters, before she steps forth
quietly to tell her story.)*

DESDEMONA
It is written—
the man is as the heavens
the woman, the earth

I waited a long time
to find it was true
I waited in silence

but then I saw him
and knew
my god walking toward me
and he
was not as other men

Power rolled from him in waves
Adventure curled along his shoulder
He spoke
and echoing murmurs
moved my blood
I looked
and could not look away

I am his wife
he, my Othello

EMILIA
But he's an Ainu

DESDEMONA
Yes, an Ainu
with quiet majesty
To me—
primeval life
still rising from the tremors
of the earth

EMILIA
Man is a god. Hmmmmh
The girl's well brought up
that would keep her in line
if the man knew his place
but I tend her and know
the balance is wronged
in her presence
this god is a child

(KI sounds. All characters swiftly exit as all banners drop from ceiling to floor. KOKEN scurry on gathering the fallen banners, and begin to "tell" their Second Ode—Love—while dancing any set pieces into place for the scene to follow, and ultimately finishing as a group, to the audience.)

KOKEN
(1)   We count
       the things we understand
       as reason

we say
the things we don't know
come from God

(2)   Our science grants us
       more command
       each day there's more
       we understand
(1)   and less we owe to God

(3)   Cloud-covered human
       stumbles his way
       up and over
       the mountain

(4)   Buddha smiles down
       wan as the sun
       wishing the way
       a lighter one

(2)   "I'll give a gift
       to humankind
       this wistful day
       I'll give
       a secret glimpse
       of heaven"

(A)   "Almighty Buddha
(1)   you open my eyes
(2)   my senses sharpen
       in chilly dawn air
(3)   my hunger delicious

(4)   my bellowing joy—
(A)   what have you sent me?

(1)   "I wake up singing
      my sleep smiles a prayer
      all and only
      because of one other
      a mortal
(A)   I love
(4)   What is this power
      Do I alone feel it?
(2)   If not I alone
      if others share
      you're growing a race
      of giants here
(3)   What do I feel?

(A)   "I love
(3)   there is a creature there
      another human, nothing rare
(3)   but now— (A) I love

(4)   "How does this creature
      fill my mind
      with joy so great
      I cannot find
      a single sorrow strong enough
      to interfere

(2)   "This other now is
      breath to me
      danger is easy

        death to me
        is clear
(2)   for now— (A) I love

(1)   "I love—and more
        as though there's no control
        of ecstacies that flood my soul
(A) my love is here"

(2)   To love
        is to receive
        a glimpse of heaven
(3)   to be allowed
        to play in heaven
        is to be a god
(1)   to mistake
        a gift from God
        for a thing you now possess
        is to risk
        the loss of heaven
(A) the loss of all
        that you were blessed
        to know (1) of God

(KI plays as KOKEN exit, revealing "bedroom" setting.
Soft lights.)

Scene 3

(EMILIA is dressing DESDEMONA for bed. At a distance, OTHELLO is removing his armor, aided by KOKEN.)

EMILIA
You have no fear?
His body hair will hang
as long as his beard
strange match
for a delicate lady

DESDEMONA
I have no fear

EMILIA
No knowing what he'll want
what he expects—
Here... A touch of scented oil
just here
where the neck curves away

DESDEMONA
In my hair?

EMILIA
Desire is cradled there

DESDEMONA
You're sure he won't be frightened

EMILIA
Of your hair?
Oh, you're teasing me

DESDEMONA
Come, is it needed?

EMILIA
Not essential
but though he is Ainu
you are one of us

DESDEMONA
Yes

EMILIA
You'll follow after
never disobedient
tend his desires
then excuse yourself
from sight
obey his parents
before your own...

He drinks warm blood of bears

DESDEMONA
How strange this speech is

EMILIA
Well, it's true

DESDEMONA
The bear is his sacred animal

EMILIA
As husband
you must give him
all your loyalty

DESDEMONA
Ohh, Emilia
are you more faithful to Iago
than to me?

EMILIA
Well...
hush now
Most important of all
you must avoid jealousy

DESDEMONA
(Laughing) Is jealousy not natural?

EMILIA
So natural for a woman
it's the greatest "do not"
on the list

DESDEMONA
I have no need
He'll take no other wives

EMILIA
Hah. So they all say
and no wise woman believes

DESDEMONA
Have you no better
things to teach me

EMILIA
About pillowing
there's a great deal
you must learn

DESDEMONA
Yes?

EMILIA
Only keep in mind—
when all is done...
it will be...
enjoyable

DESDEMONA
Oh, yes?

EMILIA
You must only be soft
and trust to...
I can't imagine
what Ainus do
that we don't too

DESDEMONA
Emilia...

EMILIA
Beneath the pillows
you'll find pictures

DESDEMONA
Pictures?

EMILIA
Diagrams—
forty-nine or so

DESDEMONA
Pictures?

EMILIA
About the bed-game
of man and woman
is there anything you know?

DESDEMONA
I know
I am the winter tree
He, the melting wind
breathes his life
into me

EMILIA
Well, yes, but...

DESDEMONA
I know bodies meet and join
so bodies will know how
Mine will join his
when he nods
whether in this drop of time
or a thousand years on
His eyes fixed on mine
hold me ready
My flesh enters his
through his eyes

(EMILIA does an I-give-up "take" to the audience, and exits, while DESDEMONA turns to face, at a distance, her new husband, OTHELLO.)

Scene 4

(Flute. Erotic LOVE DANCE.)

DESDEMONA
I'll be the earth

OTHELLO
No, the heaven

(OTHELLO and DESDEMONA dance to a tender, reclining conclusion. Anguished cry is heard from IAGO, offstage or at edge, where he's watching them. Curtain closes as IAGO moves on. KOKEN lead with lit candles.)

Scene 5

(Dark. IAGO, in candlelight downstage of curtain, speaks to audience, first holding his calm, then with bursts of fury and anguish, as he works himself toward his mad revenge.)

IAGO
I serve. Always serve
The Ainu my lord is a great man
Othello the Ainu is peerless
but she
did you see, she…
I serve, well-trained to serve
ever toiling
bright and loyal
efficient effective
ignored!

Did you see her
she stirred
Desdemona asleep was a goddess
awakened she's liquid fire

I am well-trained
I manage men well
I know how to strike
and when death will come
the angle, the blade
the flow of the blood
clean cut, exact twist

fatal...
Serve!

She is in love
she should have stayed asleep
she is in love
and I should not have seen
she is in love

Pure love burns white
and the impure go blind
at the sight of it
Ah!!
I pray
though it take my last breath
he must never have her
again *(Blows out a candle)*

But first he must burn
I will scorch his nerve
till screeching he tries
to tear himself limb from limb
Unable, he'll gasp
then laugh with relief
as he yanks a slice
through his gut

(IAGO blows out last candle. KOKEN dress IAGO in KOKEN robe. Curtain opens.)

IAGO
He'll do it himself

step after step
Now—watch all my puppets
dance on my leash

I will be served
they will serve me
all three
and the greatest of these
will be caught by the least—

(IAGO scurries up to a high place, saying—)

Here comes Cassio!

(CASSIO stalks and stumbles on—drunken, loud, with his weapon drawn. KOKEN circle and threaten him with their drawn swords. IAGO directs and manipulates them all like a puppeteer with his puppets on strings. A crazy mock dance and battle—a brawl—will begin slowly, then move faster and faster until it peaks with the entrance of OTHELLO.)

CASSIO
Clear the way
I'm coming through

IAGO
Out so late, Lieutenant?
You must be on call

CASSIO
Of course I am
(To KOKEN) Move out of my way!

IAGO
Who's in your way, Lieutenant?

CASSIO
I'll move them myself

> *(CASSIO swings wildly, slashing his weapon, heedless of danger to others.)*

IAGO
Careful, your weapon

CASSIO
Are you questioning me?
(Laughs) Iago. Old prune face

IAGO
Yes, it's me

CASSIO
A fine bottle you sent me

IAGO
It pleased you?

CASSIO
The saké—superb

IAGO
I wasn't sure it was appropriate

CASSIO
Why not

IAGO
...with the ban against drinking

CASSIO
Othello's order you mean

IAGO
He strictly laid it down

CASSIO
For those on guard

IAGO
Yes

CASSIO
How could I refuse
your kind congratulations

(KOKEN, like his conscience, veer close to CASSIO, quick, over-lapping, intimate—)

KOKEN
Buy why (A) a bottle

IAGO
Ah, yes

CASSIO
It proves you are not
jealous of my fortune

KOKEN
But what does he want

IAGO
You are on guard, you said?

CASSIO
Am I?

KOKEN
(1) You are

CASSIO
Yes, all night

IAGO
Othello trusts you then
to keep the peace

CASSIO
He does

IAGO
He's hard on his soldiers

CASSIO
They drink too much

KOKEN
As much as you?

CASSIO
They drink too much
it always leads to brawls

IAGO
Disastrous

CASSIO
Yes

IAGO
But not you, Lieutenant
You can hold your own

KOKEN
Your own
ahah
how much is that?
your own

IAGO
Tonight
Othello's room is peaceful
The battle he enjoys
sweats very sweet

CASSIO
What time is it now

IAGO
Past the call

(Rhythm picks up speed. All striking with their weapons.)

KOKEN
Past the call
You reek of alcohol

CASSIO
I told you, move on! Hah!

KOKEN
(1,4) Hiah!
(2,3) Hiah!
     We've flushed the cock
     Asss
     You're an ass
     Stroke
     Stroke again
     and paint yourself an ass
(4)   Lieutenant's in a brawl
(2)   risks a fall
(3)   past the call

CASSIO
You can't trap me

(Faster!)

KOKEN
Trap
Trap who

CASSIO
Someone must have

KOKEN
Maybe a lady
or three

CASSIO
How did this happen

KOKEN
(A)   Again!
      Joke
      Make a joke
(4)   and laugh
(2)   this is only your life
(3)   crushed in a glass
(A)   Come on, laugh
(2)   Wipe up with a smile
(3)   Make a joke
(A)   That's your style

CASSIO
I'm Captain of the guard

(Fastest! OTHELLO appears in the midst of it all, and stands witnessing the brawl. CASSIO does not see him.)

KOKEN
(4)   What guard
(2)   There's no guard here

CASSIO
Bastards!

KOKEN
How many of us can you see?

CASSIO
You'll find out who I am

KOKEN
(1)   That's the order of the day
(4)   We'll show you who you are
(2)   who are you?
(3)   you are who?

CASSIO *(Frenzy)*
I'm the Lieutenant
I second Othello

KOKEN
(1)   You follow
(A)   some fellow
(4)   We'll show you who you are
(2)   who are you?
(3)   you are who?

CASSIO
Let me be!

KOKEN
(2)   who are you?
(A)   you are who?

CASSIO
Out of my way!

(But CASSIO finds himself face to face with OTHELLO, his sword up to strike his Lord. OTHELLO draws his own sword and fights drunken CASSIO, until CASSIO sprawls—humiliated and defeated.)

CASSIO
This isn't me

OTHELLO
You are my Lieutenant no more!

(IAGO and KOKEN laugh, KI strikes, all strike Mie pose with OTHELLO.

Curtain closes.)

END OF ACT ONE

ACT TWO

Scene 1

(Flute. KI strikes. EMILIA steps out in front of curtain.)

EMILIA
Whimsy of man
flutters him belly up
snagged by the bleak wind of truth

Reason of man
slaps down his sentence
still holding his red face aloof

But no hope of man
believes truth can rule
such a fool...as Cassio

(KI strikes. KOKEN stream on with their THIRD ODE, setting the scene.)

KOKEN
(1) One day beside the mountain path
(A) a tiny crack
(1) I wander on my way
      to gathering plums

(2) One day the mountain path beside
     the crack begins
     to sway
(3) I clutch my basket close
     above my head
(A) and run

(1) Before the mountain of Othello lay
     the mountain in Othello's way
(4) An Ainu has no place
     outside his race
(1) but he built himself a tower
     climbed over their disdain
(2) climbed only with his skill
(4) his strength (3) his will
(1) till they could see
     advantage in this Ainu
(A) and gave him power

(4) Othello omnipotent
(A) Othello the great
(2) What sort does he need
     to stand in his place
     as Lieutenant?
(4) Why no sort at all
     he can please his own taste
(3) whoever appeals to his senses
(2) Cassio his opposite
     easy child of fortune
(3) reaps all things
(A) hard won (3) by Othello
(2) simply with natural grace

(1)   It could be—the mountain
        looming in Othello's way
        raised in him the sinew of the great
(4)   It could be—the riches
        unearned by Cassio
        kept him a soulless shell
(1)   It could be both know this
(A)   and still
(1)   Othello will love
        his dream form in Cassio
(A)   but hate
(1)   this hollow Cassio
(1)   who brings him (A) shame

*(KOKEN exit. IAGO signals curtain to open on a split
stage where, to one side, IAGO counsels OTHELLO; on
the other DESDEMONA meets CASSIO. When IAGO
signals the KI to strike, all his "puppets" come to life.)*

IAGO
I know you are angry
You should let him explain

OTHELLO
No, he must bear the shame
Is that so hard for your kind?

IAGO
He was your Lieutenant
There must be reason
for his action

OTHELLO
Cease!
My blade is absolute—
one slip
and he's as good as dead
The enemy in the field
will not offer him a second try

(Apart, DESDEMONA tries to speak to CASSIO.)

IAGO
Ah. but I see
the lady does not agree

OTHELLO
What?

(OTHELLO sees DESDEMONA speaking with CASSIO, but he cannot hear them. The cues overlap, between one side and the other.)

DESDEMONA
Why do you turn away?

CASSIO
I must not speak with you

DESDEMONA *(Laughs)*
What nonsense. Come here

OTHELLO
Why is she out?
The women are inside

CASSIO
Othello has shunned me

IAGO
You've granted her free movement
shall I rescind the right?

DESDEMONA
Have you made him angry?

OTHELLO   *(CASSIO hangs his head)*
And hide her from sight
like your floor-licking wives?
Of course not

(OTHELLO takes a step, and now he can hear DESDE-MONA and CASSIO, but only their <u>underlined</u> words, which the actors punch a little louder than the rest. Each scene flows on its own, but <u>tight cues</u> between the two groups are essential.)

DESDEMONA
<u>Come close</u>
<u>Speak close to my ear</u>

IAGO   *(CASSIO bends toward*
That's friendly   *DESDEMONA.)*
Perhaps she doesn't know
you have rejected him

DESDEMONA
But he loves you...

CASSIO
No longer

OTHELLO
They are friends

> DESDEMONA
> …like his brother or his son

> CASSIO
> No

IAGO
Such a generous husband
Is that wise?

> DESDEMONA
> How can I help you
> if you won't explain

OTHELLO
They are friends within my house
I am not one of you

> CASSIO
> I don't deserve your help

IAGO
What could they have to say?

> DESDEMONA
> He will be sad
> <u>What joy can there be with-
> out you?</u>

OTHELLO *(Echoes—)*
What joy

IAGO
I will stop this
Let me interrupt

OTHELLO
No. She is her own

CASSIO
He hates me now

IAGO
Something moves him

DESDEMONA
This isn't right
I'll mend your loves

IAGO
He's making some request

CASSIO
If you could, <u>I'd worship
you</u>

OTHELLO *(Echoes—)*
Worship

DESDEMONA
Of course I can
<u>Love teaches me</u>
the map of his heart

OTHELLO *(Echoes—)*
Love teaches me

IAGO
Hah! Does he grasp her hand?

CASSIO
<u>Angel</u> of mercy

*(CASSIO and DESDEMONA speak eagerly; we hear the
isolated words OTHELLO hears.)*

IAGO *(Echoes—)*
Angel

DESDEMONA
You were good to <u>come to
me</u>

OTHELLO *(Echoes—)*
Come to me

CASSIO
I only <u>want you</u> to talk to
him

IAGO *(Echoes—)*
Want

DESDEMONA
I really <u>can't wait</u>…

OTHELLO *(Echoes—)*
Can't wait

CASSIO
I've been <u>longing</u> to <u>meet
alone</u> with you

IAGO *(Echoes—)*
Longing, meet alone

DESDEMONA
<u>I'll find my way around him
Come to me tomorrow</u>

*(OTHELLO turns away, then exits. IAGO follows;
CASSIO exits another way. DESDEMONA's fan slips
through her belt/sash to the floor as she turns to exit;
EMILIA, entering, sees the fan and picks it up. She begins to call after DESDEMONA, but hesitates—)*

EMILIA *(With fan)*
My man Iago asked for this
and here—I hold it in my hand
But what do I have?
A pretty fan misled
something to tease him
and tickle my bed

My man has a secret soul
why should I mind
Even I worship
Desdemona's pure eyes
Just let him be
Before his dream breaks
he rolls over to me

(As EMILIA' smiles at audience, IAGO enters, and she teases him with the fan. FAN/DANCE SEQUENCE—as coy love play between husband and wife—she offering the fan he wants, then refusing to give it, and he caressing her in his attempts to get her to release it to him— until finally he captures it.

IAGO with the fan, waves EMILIA away and turns to audience, ecstatic—)

IAGO
Be still my joy
I have it now—
his love gift to her
so preciously
pressed to her breast
come irrepressibly...
into my hand

Oh your scent
your delicate air
come let me breathe you
conceive me in heaven

and let me rest
forever at peace

But no
My tragedy will be
I cannot keep you
My black heart
will not let me sleep
demanding I release you
my holy of holies
my sacred fan
to the careless hand
of the least worthy man!

So let it work!
Let your beauties be bent
to my desecrate plan
to mid-wife a monster—
that's my evil intent
for this fan

So go!

> *(IAGO hides the fan behind his back, and, as CASSIO promenades past him, IAGO SLIPS THE FAN into CASSIO's belt, and hurries away.*
>
> *CASSIO alone, finds the fan, laughs, wondering which lady slipped it to him, flips it open, admiring, and plays with it, while...*

IAGO brings OTHELLO to a place where he can watch CASSIO unseen, then IAGO moves casually to meet CASSIO.)

IAGO
You're more cheerful
Lieutenant
than when we last met

CASSIO
My hopes have lifted it's true

(CASSIO happily flutters the fan. OTHELLO, seeing it, is astonished.)

OTHELLO
Nooo…

IAGO
What's this? It's beautiful

CASSIO
Yes, isn't it

IAGO
And delicate
A gentle lady's I'm sure

CASSIO *(Laughs)*
Gentle?
I'm not so sure
She left it with me

IAGO
Aha!
Near your bed?

CASSIO
I know what I'll do
I'll make a present of it

IAGO
To another lady
who will be pleased?

CASSIO
Oh yes, she'll thank me

IAGO
And offer her own gift coyly?

(CASSIO laughs, and mimes a woman's suggestive moves.)

CASSIO
Oh yes, like so…
But then like so

IAGO
"Let me repay you, kind Cassio"

(IAGO and CASSIO laugh and move off. OTHELLO is tortured.)

OTHELLO
She didn't give it away
young wives must not give gifts
The fan of my mother
first gift to my bride
it isn't gone
it's not the one
it must not be the same
Fan of my mother
dyed through a thousand nights
colors of earth and moon
mystic powers blended
to hold love secure
"Give this to your love, my son
so long as she has it
she binds your love sure"

(As OTHELLO exits, DESDEMONA and EMILIA enter, searching.)

DESDEMONA
It must be somewhere
look more carefully
It has value for him
nearly magical
When did you last see it?

EMILIA
When did I? I think
you had it yesterday
when you saw Cassio

DESDEMONA
When I saw Cassio
Yes. I tucked it at my waist
It must have fallen through

EMILIA
It must have fallen through

DESDEMONA
Look everywhere
Quickly, do it now
I could never bear
to tell him that it's gone

    (DESDEMONA moves away; EMILIA is left alone.)

EMILIA
I would never dare
to tell her *where*
it's gone
What have I done?
Such a whim of his
Why did I aid his trail
I should have let it lie
His wit jumps ahead of mine
if not, the game would stale

    (EMILIA exits.

    *OTHELLO enters, ranging across the stage—a prowling,
howling demon.*

IAGO comes to whisper to him, but OTHELLO tries to shake him off...)

OTHELLO
I have a nightmare
in my waking mind
They're always at it—"he and she"

(...as CASSIO and DESDEMONA appear—as though in OTHELLO's mind—performing a surreal DUMB-SHOW of the Imagination over which KOKEN dangle and flutter the magical FAN on a flexible rod. First the couple's moves are demure, but gradually they suggest love-making, perhaps under a kimono.)

IAGO
But this that I tell you
did happen

OTHELLO
You say he was sleeping?

IAGO
Yes, asleep
beside the campfire

OTHELLO
And you heard him speak

IAGO
First he moved his leg

OTHELLO
He moved...

IAGO
...his leg
I felt his knee
along my thigh

OTHELLO
And Cassio said...

IAGO
It was more a moan
very low and barely clear
I heard—Desdemona

OTHELLO
Desdemona?

IAGO
Desdemona come now
quietly. We must hide
our love. Come now
turn again to me.

OTHELLO
Again

IAGO
Again

OTHELLO
Again!

IAGO
Again

(OTHELLO finally screams from the intensity, moving forward, and his tortured vision [DESDEMONA with CASSIO] disappears from his mind [curtain can close behind him], but KOKEN now surround and guide OTHELLO through his DEMON TRANSFORMATION:)

KOKEN
(A)   Come this way
         you're almost there
         we'll take you
         come it's easy
         ease into (1) nothing
(2)   nothing
(3)   nothing
         nothing will soothe

OTHELLO
Since first I felt her gaze
I've known she was mine
then what is this pain
how did it rise
and all over nothing...
Ah, fool, don't you know
this "nothing" is where
love's language resides?

I know, oh I know
the flutter of lashes takes
only an instant
love's presence is known
with one sweep of the room
no need for a touch
no answering smile
my iron gaze watches for passion
She and He—
passion moves without speaking
love gathers force in free air
till their spirits climb strong
to the top of the room
boldly laugh at the throng
standing helpless below
and lustfully couple there!

(IAGO moves in front of OTHELLO, hiding him [perhaps with black cloth] as OTHELLO sinks to his knees to be transformed.)

KOKEN
Hold very still
and maybe it will pass
Old stories tell
of all the ghosts
that bring disaster
there's only one we fear
before the person dies
and that is (A) jealousy

Livid dreams at night
will take you
raging into hell
you go insane
without a cause
without a cure
Like lust
this rage is whetted
by the carnage it performs
you may not even realize
your (A) crimes

*(IAGO drops down as OTHELLO stands up in DEMON
WIG.)*

OTHELLO
What is it?
Othello the strong man
is trembling
No! Othello is steady
trained from a babe
not only for hunt
trained also for wisdom
reasoned debate
by the fire
seasoned by tongues
dipped in song
Then why this trembling
what is wrong?

(IAGO applies Demon Make-up to OTHELLO's face.)

KOKEN
(2)   To love
(A)   is to receive
        a glimpse of heaven
(3)   to be allowed
        to play in heaven
(A)   is to be a god
(1)   to mistake
        a gift from God
(1)   for a thing (A) you now possess
(1)   is to risk
        the loss of heaven
(A)   the loss of all
        that you were blessed
(A)   to know (1) of God

OTHELLO
What is it—
Help me!
No! Don't cry
Be still

(OTHELLO Demon transformation proceeds...)

There's Cassio
a soldier raised by me
to his Lieutenantcy
and now...
Consider quietly!
Then there's my wife
what wife!
My wife I love

then why...
She sought my love
then why!

My peace lies strangled now
I cannot breathe

> *(KOKEN pull Hikinuki—[trick strings] so that OTHELLO's outside costume drops revealing his under-dressed costume and transforming OTHELLO into a Demon.)*

KOKEN
- (4) Breathe
- (A) you can breathe
- (2) Give it up
- (3) The man that you were
        wants to cling to you
- (4) Breathe (A) you can breathe
- (1) The demon that you are
        is sheer power
- (4) Breathe
- (A) and be born!

> *(Transformation of OTHELLO is complete. He stands as a DEMON. KOKEN move away.)*

OTHELLO
My nerve ends now
are patched with ice and fire
Go round me now
there's no way past

White hot spikes probe
the pit of my brain
a billion cells rise molten
in a heaving mass
This pain won't last
it can't last
it won't last

KOKEN
(1)   Still (A) hold still
(1)   no more fear
        you see the worst
(2)   the worst is here
(1)   you stand in fire
        and still survive
(A)   you've met the ghost
        that is alive

(KOKEN exit.)

Scene 2

(Curtain may open. OTHELLO stands as Demon on one side; DESDEMONA kneels on her "bed" [platform] on the other side [perhaps a screen between]. Both face audience—she does not see his demon appearance.)

DESDEMONA
My dear lord
I am afraid for you

OTHELLO *(Gasps)*
Desdemona

DESDEMONA
Something tortures you
I cannot see

OTHELLO
Oh Desdemona

DESDEMONA
Please let me help you
Let me touch your wet brow

OTHELLO
Please...

DESDEMONA
Come to me
Come to me come to me

OTHELLO
Oh yes

DESDEMONA
I know what hurts you
it is hurting him too

OTHELLO
Him...

DESDEMONA
He's tortured
by the same pain as you

OTHELLO
He…

DESDEMONA
Forgive Cassio

OTHELLO
Cassio

DESDEMONA
Forgive Cassio

OTHELLO
No

DESDEMONA
Forgive Cassio

(OTHELLO screams, then recovers.)

DESDEMONA
My lord

OTHELLO
This friend of yours
This…Cassio
has wronged me too far

DESDEMONA
No friend of mine

OTHELLO
No? You deny him

DESDEMONA
I deny
all that displeases you

OTHELLO
You deny all...

DESDEMONA
Can I have a friend
who is not yours?

OTHELLO
Who is not mine
No

DESDEMONA
But you feel how wrong you are
you refuse your soul
when you refuse to forgive
your friend Cassio

OTHELLO
Go!

DESDEMONA
What is it
please tell me

OTHELLO
I said leave me

DESDEMONA
Do you mean...

OTHELLO
Go

(DESDEMONA rises to leave, then shakes her head and returns to her knees.)

OTHELLO
A good wife would obey

DESDEMONA
Forgive me

OTHELLO
Now it's you
I must forgive
not Cassio

DESDEMONA
I cannot leave you
in pain

OTHELLO
In pain?
Are you in pain?

DESDEMONA *(Beat, then—)*
I too, yes
Have I done
something to you

OTHELLO
What could you do
You are my loyal wife

DESDEMONA
Yes

OTHELLO
I'm married to you

DESDEMONA
Yes

OTHELLO
You serve me in everything
move by my hand
obey my command

DESDEMONA
You know I do

OTHELLO
And the fan?

DESDEMONA
What...

OTHELLO
Where is the fan?
Hah! Gone!
Gone with all that was sacred
all that was mine
Then you go too!
Go unfold and bend for Cassio

DESDEMONA
My lord

OTHELLO
For Cassio!

DESDEMONA
I open my breast
please strike
if I can ease you
by dying again
I died once
only feeling your pain

OTHELLO
Desdemona

DESDEMONA
Please come to me
Let me help you

OTHELLO
Desdemona
a whore...

DESDEMONA
No...no

OTHELLO
You're a whore

> *(OTHELLO leaves, DESDEMONA shocked silent, sinks to the ground; IAGO enters, kneels near her.)*

DESDEMONA
Iago...help me
you must help me
regain him
the pain
is too great
You must prove me true

IAGO
Whose pain, honored lady?
What do you think
you can teach me
of pain
None is greater
than mine for you

> *(DESDEMONA alarmed, collapses. Curtain closes.)*

Scene 3

*(DANCE OF DEATH—dream killing of everyone by
OTHELLO, the raging demon. CHARACTERS make a
moving line, one behind the other, or stretched like a
menacing caterpillar with many tentacles. As OTHELLO
attacks, they falter and rise again.)*

KOKEN
(1)　Livid (1,4) dreams at night
(1)　will take you raging into hell
(4)　you go insane (1) without a cause
(4)　without a cure
(1)　Like lust
　　　this rage is whetted
　　　by the carnage it performs
(4)　you may not even realize
(1,4)　your crimes.

(1)　Hold very still
(4)　and maybe it will pass
(1)　Old stories tell
　　　of all the ghosts
　　　that bring disaster
　　　there's only one we fear
　　　before the person dies
(4)　and that is (1,4) jealousy

(1)　Still (1,4) hold still
(1,4)　no more fear
　　　you see the worst
　　　the worst is here

you stand in fire
and still survive
you've met the ghost
that is alive

Dreams will take you
Dreams will take you

(Conclusion of Dance—when OTHELLO has "killed" them all, the CHARACTERS laugh hysterically at his madness as they back away; he runs off. Curtain opens.)

Scene 4

(Bedroom. Armor displayed. EMILIA preparing DESDE-MONA for bed, who is very quiet.)

DESDEMONA
This jealousy
is a fearful thing

EMILIA
It's a worthless thing
that I'm sure

DESDEMONA
Do you know what it is, Emilia?

EMILIA
Hah. It isn't allowed us

what good would it do
Women must care for each other

DESDEMONA
Is Iago jealous of you?

EMILIA
Oho! Like a dog with his tail

DESDEMONA
Does it frighten you

EMILIA
No. You just fix a fierce eye
and tell him he lies

DESDEMONA
Who would lie about me, Emilia

EMILIA
No human. And no creature at peace

DESDEMONA
This jealousy
does not breathe
the same air
as love

EMILIA
Many say they are the same

DESDEMONA
Poor Cassio
I may have killed him
when I wanted to heal

EMILIA
Poor poor Cassio
Now there's a fair bit of meat
If Iago were not jealous
don't you think
I'd take a turn
for such a treat

DESDEMONA
You are laughing
That's good
When it's over
tomorrow
my headdress is yours
Take it now

EMILIA *(Alarmed)*
Dear lady...

DESDEMONA
Come help me
I'll wear
my wedding night kimono

(Sings) The willow dips her trailing hair
        into a silent pool

she sees herself reflected there
and moans "how cruel, so cruel"
The willow longs to feel the breeze
caress her trailing hair
He gently spreads her to receive
the lovers hiding there

Go now. He'll be here soon

(Sings) Oh come to me, together we
      will weave a summer tune
      instead of waiting helplessly
      for winter's frozen moon

Don't look so alarmed
You've forgotten this tie

EMILIA
What do you mean?

DESDEMONA
What do I mean, how?

EMILIA
What do you mean
...with the headdress

DESDEMONA
He called me whore, Emilia

EMILIA
It's his madness
It means nothing!

DESDEMONA
Nothing…
and everything

EMILIA
That some worm has
primed him to say it
does not make it true

DESDEMONA
He says
and believes it

EMILIA
With whom!
Who is accused?

DESDEMONA
I don't know
but I fear for
your pretty Cassio

EMILIA
My Cassio
rot Cassio!
It's a lie
a filthy lie
it can't stain

your angel soul
You married a beast
spit on his race
It cancels your vow
you owe him
no faith

DESDEMONA
You can't make me angry
Emilia
not now

*(IAGO enters and draws OTHELLO on like a puppet-
master, with KOKEN, who behave like a pack of judges,
behind him.)*

DESDEMONA
My love
I wait for you

KOKEN
(1) You are accused
         of breaking the thread
         of married truth
(2) You are accused
         of turning toward
         another
(3) of offering your body
         to some other
(A) for his use

EMILIA
And this other
has he no name?

KOKEN
(4)   He is a man
        the same
        as other men

DESDEMONA
"My god
is not as other men"

KOKEN
(A)   You stand condemned

EMILIA
What's the evidence!

KOKEN
(1)   What do you say?

EMILIA
Who has denounced her
on what evidence

DESDEMONA
I deny
the man
and any other
than Othello
my lord

KOKEN
She denies

DESDEMONA
But I accept
the sentence
and will willingly
carry it out
on his sword

EMILIA
What sentence
Answer me!

KOKEN
(A)   She denies
(4)   but accepts
(1)   denies
        but accepts
        the sentence
        etched in gold
        on her fan

(IAGO is moving toward EMILIA; but she doesn't see him.)

EMILIA
The fan! No!
The fan?
I took it
I did it
the blame is all mine

(Frantic) Iago. Where is it?
Where is he?
I'll tell you
Listen to me!

    (IAGO stabs EMILIA.)

DESDEMONA
I accept the sentence
since he believes I lie
If he can look at me
and believe me untrue
then I know love can die
and so will I
easily

    *(DESDEMONA lies down on the bed. OTHELLO stands
    above her, at its head.)*

OTHELLO
I proceed
as on another night
when wind did not breathe
from fear to disturb us
(Chokes) oh, love!

KOKEN
(1) Proceed
      and the pain will cease *[repeats]*

    *(KOKEN surround the bed; as scene proceeds they draw
    out strands of extremely long hair and circle DESDE-*

MONA, interweaving the strands, winding them close around her neck, and while OTHELLO reminds himself of their life together, the KOKEN urge him to strangle her. OTHELLO's lines are like an obbligato above the KOKENS' seamless murmuring wave of sound—)

OTHELLO
My limbs moved
in low-chiming space
pulled through a void
to your arms

KOKEN
(1) She's only bewitchment
(2) She's not of this earth
     Remember nothing *[repeats]*

OTHELLO
Soft petals of breath
fill the room
where she lingers...

KOKEN
(3) She split your skull
(4) She poured in demons
     Remember nothing *[repeats]*

OTHELLO
A wisp of her laughter
eases the dark
Her fresh-lit eyes
assure me of dawn

KOKEN *(Continuous repeat)*
(A)   Remember nothing, remember nothing...

OTHELLO
Her touch is silk water
lapping my flesh
surging my blood
past the rim of forgetting

KOKEN
(1)   Straight into hell
(2)   down to hell
      you're in hell

OTHELLO
No...

KOKEN *(Moving away)*
(3)   Save your life
      Strike now!

OTHELLO *(Screams)*
Noooo!

   (OTHELLO strangles DESDEMONA; she is dead.

   Then he collapses, still staring; like a stone that, finally,
   speaks—)

OTHELLO
Stone washed white
by lashing sea

baked pure
by the sheer cut of sun
Stone smoothed round
on the way to sand
the way all life must run

(Blackout, or light change.)

Scene 5
EPILOGUE

(OTHELLO standing over DESDEMONA. All other CHARACTERS stand facing audience.)

EMILIA
It happened in a time
such things could happen
not so very long ago

KOKEN
(2) The Karma of each
      winding its way to fulfillment
      is sometimes called Fate
(1) Some are driven towards it
(3) but some merely stroll
(A) aimlessly

CASSIO
Imagine my astonishment
to hear myself named
Commander

new General
Lord Cassio!
It's true Iago has more skill
but the scandal—
his fresh wife-killing
well...

IAGO *(Cutting CASSIO off)*
The woman was hysterical
my wife went mad

CASSIO
Desdemona deserved her death
no more than I
deserve this fortune of mine
Othello was maddened by passion
it can rage uncontrolled in the great
Amazingly, he stands alive

IAGO
Death is not punishment for Ainu

KOKEN
(1) He seems to you alive?
     He is the ghost (A) that is alive

CASSIO *(Proclaiming)*
Let all acknowledge—
in questions of life and death
the matter of when and who
will be answered by Fate

IAGO
Karma, hah! What is it?
That after managing all
I planned
I must bend again
at the heel of Cassio?
No! Begin again:
a new goal I can never achieve
that's my object
the mischief that falls in my way
that is Fate

EMILIA
No!
They were beauty and beast
each so unlike
unable to fathom the other
She desired
his mastering fire
while her life-song
raised longing in him
to belong

Pure love burns white
and the impure go blind
at the sight of it

We long for pure love—
a rose in new snow—
and know that on earth
it cannot be
but such was she

Desdemona
and he could be moved
to totally love
because he was as childlike
as she

KOKEN
(1)   To totally love
        is exposure complete
        a scalpel that opens the heart
        When beating life lies
        so exposed
        a speck introduced
        can be lethal
(3)   Their lethal speck
        was a treacherous lie
(4)   so grotesque (A) so infectious
(3)   it was futile to try
        to resist it

EMILIA
And I too, I
went blind at the sight
laid my own careless strand
in the web *(Flicks out the fan)*
And she is dead

*(EMILIA bitterly flutters fan around IAGO, reminiscent
of their fan dance. He is like stone, does not respond.)*

EMILIA
Fate, he says

He says I fell on his knife
and so died at his hand
What is true
let the story unfold:
the demon I married
alone rolled
the wheel of Fate
and that wheel has gathered us all
but the men stand alive
while the women
are spread underfoot
as it ever was
of old

(IAGO mimes stabbing EMILIA, who collapses and lies down beside DESDEMONA.)

KOKEN

(1) Mankind fights
    in a narrow pass
    without a view
    of the soul

(2) Who would strike
    another who sees
    that each is part
    of the whole

(4) Do not desire
    to do more than borrow
(3) the fruits of the earth
    or its sorrow

(4)   Remain as a child
(2)   in wonder (A) and love
(3)   desire nothing
       and all things
(A)   will follow

(Curtain closes.

Curtain opens—entire company in tableau, strike final Mie pose. Lights out. Lights up...

Blackout.)

THE END

The Willow

Words and Music by Karen Sunde

Quickly Flowing ♩= 120

The wil-low dips her trail - ing hair in-to a si - lent pool.

She sees her-self re-flect-ed there and moans how cruel, so cruel.

The wil-low longs to feel the breeze ca-ress her trail-ing hair.

He gent-ly spreads her to re-ceive the lov-ers hid-ing there. Oh

come to me to-geth-er we will weave a sum-mer tune in-stead of wait-ing

help-less-ly for win - ter's fro - zen moon.

MISSION 3

TIME BOMB

MISSION 3

TIME BOMB

SIGMUND BROUWER

TYNDALE
KIDS

TYNDALE HOUSE PUBLISHERS, INC.
WHEATON, ILLINOIS

CHAPTER 1

On the side of the cliff, I hung from a thin metal cable. Hundreds of feet below me, the jagged red rocks of the Martian valley floor pointed up at me like deadly spears.

The temperature had risen from minus one hundred degrees Fahrenheit to a nice, warm minus 20 degrees Fahrenheit. Wind pushed at my body, making me sway from side to side. But it could have been worse. I could have been stuck in a sandstorm, with grains of sand hitting me at 60 miles an hour, rattling off my titanium shell and blinding me completely.

As it was, I had a good view. On Mars, at midday, when the sand isn't blowing, the sun is blue against a butterscotch-colored sky. The clouds are barely more than stretched-out strings of fog, lighter blue than the sun.

I could look across the entire valley and see the oranges and reds of Martian soil. Nearly 10 miles away, a gigantic dome held all two hundred of the scientists and tekkies who founded the first colony on Mars. Under that dome was oxygen and water and warmth and food (all the things humans needed to survive).

Out here? There was no oxygen. No water. No warmth. And no food.

And, of course, those jagged rocks waited for any mistakes. From where I was, it wouldn't matter much that gravity on Mars is about a third of Earth's gravity. If my grip on the cable slipped, those rocks would tear through my robot body like daggers. What made it worse was that I had a passenger strapped onto my back.

My job was to make it to the bottom of the cliff with both of us undamaged.

At the top, the metal cable was attached to a long spike driven deep into the soil. All three hundred feet of the cable dangled from this spike.

I held on to the cable with a gripper in each hand. Each gripper clamped the cable securely with much more power than I could have gotten just by using my fingers.

The trick was to unclamp the gripper in my right hand and hold on with the gripper in my left hand. Then I had to bring my free right hand down and reclamp at a level below my left hand. Once the right-hand grip was secure, I unclamped the left and reclamped it below the right. And so on. It was slow work that took a lot of concentration.

One thing made this easier. My lower body was on wheels, so all I had to do was let myself roll down the cliff. Slowly. Very slowly.

I was halfway down when it happened.

As I leaned against the cliff, my right wheel hit a loose portion of rock. It broke away, clattering down the cliff. My right side swung inward, spinning me sideways.

This wouldn't have been a problem if I'd been clamping the cable with both grippers. But I was only holding with my left gripper.

In panic, I grabbed at the cable with my right hand.

Because I was spinning, I missed the cable and jammed my hand into the cliff. This pushed me away from the cliff too hard. For a second, I was like a pendulum. With less gravity on Mars than on Earth, my action shot me six feet away from the side of the cliff and then banged me against rock on the return.

It felt like I'd been slammed with a baseball bat. Keeping my grip on the cable with my left hand, I fought to find the cable with my right.

But I was out of balance. Especially with a passenger on my back.

My wheels began to roll upward on the cliff wall as the weight on my back pulled me upside down and backwards.

The cable twisted more.

Still, I tried to find a grip with my right hand.

Nothing.

Then . . .

Snap.

The buckle keeping the passenger on my back opened, and suddenly I had no passenger.

"Rawling!" I shouted, as I watched the downward tumble of arms and legs. "Rawling!"

Seconds later, there was an explosion of dust as the body smashed into the rocks.

I had failed in my mission.

CHAPTER 2

I woke up blindfolded and on my back on a narrow medical bed in the computer laboratory.

"Rawling!" I called again. It had taken nearly a half hour to climb to the bottom of the cliff. And another 20 minutes to get back to the dome. Then a few minutes to get inside and park Bruce, the robot body, where it needed to be charged. "Rawling!"

Here in the lab I wore a headset, too, so I couldn't hear anything, not even my own voice as I shouted. My arms and my legs were strapped to the bed so I couldn't move. I was helpless until Rawling McTigre reached me. He was my friend, a scientist who worked with me on my virtual-reality missions.

It took a few seconds.

He lifted the blindfold, and I blinked against the lights.

Next came my headset. We did all of this because it was important that nothing distracted my mind from operating the robot body.

"Thanks," I said, glad I could see and hear through my own eyes and ears now. Not being able to do that was one of the things I didn't like about being hooked up through virtual reality to a robot. But the advantages were great, especially to a kid who was unable to use his legs. Something had gone wrong during an operation on my spine when I was too young to remember, so now I was in a wheelchair. Yet because of that and a computer link in my spine, now I was the only one who could explore the planet of Mars in a robot's body.

"You all right, Tyce?" Rawling asked, concern on his face. "The signal was clear, and I got a video feed of everything that happened."

"I'm all right," I said. "But I'm afraid if this hadn't been a test run, someone on Bruce's back would be very dead right now. That crash-test dummy you rigged really did become a crash test."

When the robot body had rolled to the base of the cliff, I'd found the dummy. It was—or had been—the weight of a human. But in the fall, the legs and arms had ripped off, and the jagged rocks had speared the body portion. I shuddered to think of what those rocks would have done to a real person.

"Mistakes are not always a bad thing," Rawling said as he unstrapped me and helped me sit up. "From what I can tell, the dummy was positioned too high. We need to strap it lower, closer to the center of gravity."

"One other thing," I said.

Rawling arched an eyebrow, the way he always did when he wanted to ask a question. He'd been a quarterback for a university back on Earth when he was younger, and his wide shoulders showed it. Now his short, dark hair was streaked with gray. One of two medical doctors under the dome, he'd also recently been appointed replacement director of the Mars Project. It might sound strange to say that though he was in his mid-40s and I was only 14 (in Earth years),

Rawling was a great friend. After all, until a month ago I'd been the only kid under the dome out of two hundred people here, so I didn't expect friends my age. Also, Rawling had worked with me for hours every day since I was eight, training me in a virtual-reality program to control a robot body as if it were my own.

"You don't need to worry about the strap," I continued. "That's not why the dummy fell away from me."

Rawling arched his eyebrow again.

"It's the buckle," I said. I pictured how it had opened. "While I was swinging, it banged into a piece of rock. That's what released it. You need some sort of safety guard on it."

"Good point," Rawling said. "Very good point. I'll get one of the tekkies to make the changes right away."

Right away? What was his rush? I wondered. Today was supposed to be a normal school day for me, and Rawling had asked me to take time off to learn cliff climbing.

"Rawling?"

"Yes?" Rawling lifted my legs off the bed and helped me into my nearby wheelchair.

"Why are we doing this?" I asked. "I mean, you don't expect that someday I'll actually have to lug someone down a cliff . . ."

Rawling didn't answer. Instead, he walked over to the computer and the transmitter and began to shut down the power.

"Rawling?"

He finally turned to me.

"Tyce Sanders," he said in a strange tone, "meet me in my office in five minutes."

CHAPTER 3

Until recently, the director's office had belonged to someone else. (For more on that story, see my first diary, *Mission 1: Oxygen Level Zero.*) In the month since he'd taken over as director, Rawling had been so busy that he hadn't made any changes yet. The framed paintings of Earth scenes, like sunsets and mountains, still hung on the walls. Blaine Steven, the former director, had spent a lot of the government's money to get those luxuries included in the cargo shipped to Mars. But even a director didn't get bookshelves and real books. Cargo was too expensive. If people wanted books, they read them on DVD-gigarom.

Usually I admired the framed paintings because no one else in the dome had them. This time, however, my attention was on Rawling.

"Tyce," Rawling said from behind his desk, "I don't want to believe what I think I'm seeing."

"You're seeing me," I said with a grin. He seemed so serious that I wanted to lighten him up. "What's hard to believe about that? You called for me five minutes ago, and here I am."

"Very, very funny," he said. No grin. "Let me get you a

9

microphone and a crowd so they can throw tomatoes at you."

"Tomatoes?"

As the only human ever born on Mars, I'd never been to Earth. But I knew tomatoes were something people on Earth grew and ate. I'd seen photos of them on my DVD-gigarom encyclopedia, but I'd never tasted them. And I sure couldn't figure out why people would throw them at me.

"It's an old Earth thing," Rawling explained, obviously wishing he hadn't started this. "When they don't like a comedian or an actor, they throw rotten vegetables at him."

"Hmm," I said. "You sure tomatoes are vegetables? Some people argue that—"

"Not now, Tyce," he groaned. "Please, not now."

Rawling stood and walked around his desk to where I sat in my wheelchair.

"These are digital photos from the satellite," he said, waving sheets of paper at me. Rawling meant the communications satellite that circled Mars. "And if I'm seeing what I believe I'm seeing, you've got to promise to keep this absolutely secret. I'll be making a public report as soon as possible, but until then . . ."

He handed the photographs to me.

I studied them. Mars has nearly zero cloud cover, so unless a gigantic sandstorm is brewing, the satellite takes very clear photographs. They are sent by radio transmission to a computer here under the dome, then digitally translated into printouts of photos of the planet's surface.

What I saw in the photographs were different shots of a valley. In real life, the soil would be red and brown and orange. The black-and-white digital printouts just showed different shades of gray. The satellite had provided long shots and close-up shots, all taken from directly overhead, some five miles above the surface of the planet.

"Wow," I said. "Rocks and more rocks. This looks so scary I don't think my heart can take it."

Rawling sighed and squatted beside my wheelchair. "That," he said, pointing to a black, square rock in the center of one of the close-up photos, "is what's truly scary."

Sensing he'd had enough of my joking around, I didn't make any more dumb remarks.

"Notice how absolutely smooth and square that rock is," Rawling said.

Now that he mentioned it, I could see it was.

"You can't tell from the photo, but it's about the size of this office," he continued. "Now keep looking. You'll see several more."

He was right. In the jumble of boulders in the valley, I counted four more of those strangely smooth, strangely square gigantic rocks.

"You've got me interested," I said. "What are they? How did they get there?"

"Not so fast," Rawling said firmly. He paced for a few seconds, then stopped. "First question. Why haven't we seen them before? I mean, our satellite has been circling Mars ever since the dome was established almost 15 Earth years ago. Suddenly this."

I thought of yesterday's big event. A rumble had shaken the dome. It felt like an earthquake—marsquake—had occurred miles and miles away. Or like an asteroid had banged into Mars. Although no damage had been done, it had rattled things briefly, and it was all anyone could talk about—scientists in their labs, tekkies running the experiments for the scientists, me, Mom, Dad, and my new friend, Ashley Jordan.

"First answer," I guessed. "It has something to do with that explosion we felt yesterday."

"Exactly. There's a lot of Martian soil now exposed to the surface that wasn't there before yesterday. In other words, those square black things were buried."

"I give up," I said. "What are they? How did they get there?"

Rawling shook his head. "All I can tell you is I'm nearly 100 percent certain those black things aren't a natural part of Mars."

"They couldn't have come from Earth," I reasoned. "Otherwise we'd know about them already, right? I mean, the Mars Project is the first time anyone from Earth has landed on Mars. And if no one from Earth put them there . . ."

I stopped, too afraid to say out loud what I was thinking: *If no one from Earth had put them there, who had done it?*

Rawling read my mind. He nodded. "Now you understand why I don't want to believe what I think I'm seeing."

"Now I understand," I answered.

"Which is why I called you here," Rawling said slowly— as if he wished he hadn't had to call me into his office.

"Yes?" I asked.

"Tyce, you can say no if you don't want to do it."

"No to what?"

"It's absolutely *imperative* that we take a closer look at those things. The trouble is, it won't be as easy as a practice run. Not considering where we need to go." That's when Rawling went over his plan with me, step by step.

CHAPTER 4

"Why is there something instead of nothing?" Ashley asked me, hand on her right hip in her trademark thinking pose.

I'd promised Rawling I'd return to work with him after talking through his plan with my mom, Kristy, a leading plant biologist, and my dad, Chase, an interplanetary pilot. But first I'd wheeled across half of the dome to return to where Ashley and I had been studying some math questions.

Since the dome's total area was about the size of four Earth football fields, I never had to travel far. Besides the small, plastic mini-domes of the scientists and tekkies, there were experimental labs and open areas where equipment was maintained. The main level of the two-story dome held the mini-domes and laboratories. One level up, a walkway about 10 feet wide circled the inside of the dome walls. People mostly used the walkway for jogging. Not me, of course. The tekkies had built a ramp for my wheelchair so I could access the second level, and then the third and smallest level by a narrow catwalk.

Centered at the top of the dome, this third level was only 15 feet wide. On its deck a powerful telescope perched beneath a round bubble of clear glass that stuck up from the black glass that formed the rest of the dome. From there, the massive telescope gave an incredible view of the solar system.

This was my home, and I loved it. And it was even better now that I had a friend my age. A month ago Ashley Jordan had arrived on the most recent spaceship with her father, Dr. Shane Jordan, an artificial-intelligence computer expert. Like me, she was a science freak. Even better, she was fun to be around—even if she did ask strange questions. *Something instead of nothing?*

"Something what?" I asked. "Nothing where? I thought we were going to work on calculus."

It was midafternoon. We sat in an open area near the gardens, with the giant curved ceiling of the dome stretching in all directions. It was quiet here, with only the occasional conversations of passing scientists or tekkies to interrupt us.

"Calculus." She made a face, as if she'd tasted something awful. "More fun to daydream." Pointing to her handheld computer, she continued. "And I was getting tired of the teacher. That monotone voice is enough to drive you crazy."

I nodded. I knew what she meant. I'd learned most of my school stuff through DVD-gigarom too. When I was little, I'd actually talked in a monotone for a while because I thought the voices on the computer were from real people.

"So you began to daydream," I said. "About nothing? Or something?"

For years, I'd envied Earth kids because when they went to school, they could talk to someone. Now, finally, even though it was only a classroom of two, I was in school too. Even if the conversation didn't make much sense. "This universe," Ashley said, pointing upward through the ceiling of the dome. "Solar system. Mars. Earth. Sun. Why should all of this stuff be here? Why not nothing?"

I peered closely at her. With her black hair cut short and a serious look on her face, she appeared older than 13. And because her dark brown, almond-shaped eyes could be very unreadable, it was sometimes difficult to figure out if she was joking.

Like now. I waited for her to light up with a big grin, which, when it happened, would change her from mysterious to tomboyish.

"Well . . . ," she said impatiently. She pressed her lips together and squinted at me. "I'm waiting for an answer."

So she wasn't joking.

"Try to picture nothing," she said when all I did was scratch my head.

"Sure," I said. I thought for a second. "Done."

"No," she said. "I disagree. You didn't picture nothing."

I held up my hands in protest. "You can't disagree! You don't even know what I was thinking!"

"Whatever you were thinking was wrong," she said. "You *can't* picture nothing."

"But—"

"You can picture an empty jar. Or maybe a big room with nothing in it. Or even all the space between the stars. But whenever you picture nothing, don't you picture something that's holding all that nothing?"

"Well, maybe I—"

"So why should there be something instead of nothing? You know, all the stuff that makes the stars and the planets. Why can't there be nothing? And where did the something come from? Did it exist forever? But how can something exist forever? But if first there was nothing, how did it suddenly become something? I mean, you don't make rocks the size of a planet from empty air. Then think about all the stars and planets in the entire universe. Those came from nothing? Ha! And—"

"Ashley!" I said. "You're making me dizzy."

Finally she grinned. "I'm making myself dizzy."

"At least we agree on *something*."

She nodded, and her tiny silver cross earrings flashed. She reached up to touch them. "I think it's cool to spend time wondering about God and Jesus and why we're put into this universe."

I returned her nod. It *was* cool. There are so many mysteries that science is so far from figuring out, and yet God knows about them. A person could spend a lifetime thinking about God and everything he's done and never get bored.

Ashley closed her handheld computer. "I'm done for the day. How about you?"

I thought of what Rawling had asked me to do. How he'd made me promise not to tell anyone except my parents.

"Me too," I said. "At least my schoolwork. We've done enough this week that we're ahead, right?"

Ashley nodded again. "Right. Let's go see how Flip and Flop are doing."

Flip and Flop are the little koala-type animals that she and I had rescued from a genetics experiment gone wrong. And just in the nick of time, too. (To read more about it, see my second diary, *Mission 2: Alien Pursuit*.) It hadn't taken long for the tekkies at the dome to adopt the friendly creatures as mascots.

"Wish I could," I said, "but I need to ask my parents something."

Ashley shrugged. "See you tonight, then? At the tele-scope?"

"Sure," I said.

I just hoped—after everything else Rawling had told me—that tonight wouldn't be my last time to see Ashley . . . or anyone else, for that matter.

CHAPTER 5

An hour later, I sat in front of my computer in my room in the mini-dome I shared with my parents. Aside from my desk, there was a bed. Not much else. Under the dome, everybody wore the standard uniform—a navy blue jumpsuit—so I didn't need a big closet. And because I was always in a wheelchair, I didn't need a chair.

My computer was what made the room alive for me. Through it I learned about Earth, played computer games, and listened to music, even if most of the songs were 10 years old. And when the solar system was clear of the electromagnetic particles from solar flares, I could even pick up some Internet transmissions. Although my body was in the prison of a wheelchair, my mind could go almost anywhere.

Tonight, though, I wasn't going to listen to music or read DVD-gigarom books. It had been a week or two since I'd written anything in my journal.

I flicked on the power, and my computer booted up faster than I could count to five. I clicked the right spots, and my writing program opened up.

I began to keyboard my thoughts into my computer diary. . . .

A short while ago, it looked like the entire Mars colony wasn t going to survive because the dome s oxygen level was dropping (see *Mission 1: Oxygen Level Zero*, my first diary). At the time, I agreed to write a diary so people on Earth would know about those last days from the viewpoint of a kid instead of a scientist.

We all survived, of course, and I decided to keep a diary by describing things that happen under the dome. Sometimes I m too tired to get on my computer to write like this. Other times there doesn t seem to be much to write about, so I spend time up at the telescope.

But with what I ve just learned from Rawling, it looks like I d better not be lazy with my journal. Sometimes I pretend I m writing a letter to myself, so that when I m an old man, I can read these letters and remember what it was like to be the first person born on Mars. After all, everybody was surprised when my mother and father fell in love with each other on their eight-month journey to Mars 15 years ago. Once on the planet, they exchanged vows over a radio-phone with a preacher on Earth. Then, an Earth year later, the director of the Project, Blaine Steven, was even more shocked when my mom announced she was going to have a baby. It made things really compli- cated since ships arrive here only every three years, and cargo space is very, very expensive. There was no room for baby items or a motorized wheelchair.

But you don t have to feel sorry for me. Because of the operation on my spine that went wrong, I m

able to explore Mars and the universe in a way no
human in history has ever been able to do by
controlling a robot body. The way it works is . . .

I stopped my keyboarding and let my mind wander to all
I was able to do as I controlled the robot body. As I thought
about Bruce, I reached down to the small pouch hanging
from the armrest of my wheelchair. Pulling out three red
balls, I began to juggle, keeping all three in the air. Juggling
didn't take much concentration for me. Especially since the
gravity was lower on Mars than on Earth.

I kept the red balls in the air for another five minutes, remembering the first time I had sent the robot body outside
the dome. Because Bruce delivered sights and sounds and
sensations to my mind, it was almost like being outside in
my very own body. Although the computer effects were very
complicated, the theory was simple.

I stopped juggling the red balls and began to describe it
for my diary.

In virtual reality, you put on a surround-sight
helmet that gives you a three-dimensional view of
a scene on a computer program. The helmet is
wired so that when you turn your head, it directs
the computer program to shift the scene as if you
were there in real life. Sounds generated by the
program reach your ears, making the scene seem
even more real. Because you're wearing a wired
jacket and gloves, the arms and hands you see in
your surround-sight picture move wherever you
move your own arms and hands.

But here's what you might not have thought
about when it comes to virtual reality: when you

take off the surround-sight helmet and the jacket and gloves that are wired to a computer, you re actually still in a virtual-reality suit. Your body.

Rawling was the one who explained it best to me.

You see, your brain doesn't see anything. It doesn't hear anything. It doesn't smell anything. It doesn't taste anything. It doesn't feel anything. Instead, it takes all the information that's delivered to it by your nerve endings from your eyes, ears, nose, tongue, skin, or bones, and translates that information.

In other words, the body is like an amazing 24-hour-a-day virtual-reality suit that can power itself by eating food and heal itself when parts get cut or broken. It moves on two legs, has two arms to pick things up, and is equipped to give information through all five senses. Except instead of taking you through virtual reality, a made-up world, your body takes you through the real world.

What if your brain could be wired directly into a robot? Then wouldn't you be able to see, hear, and do everything the robot could?

Well, that's me. The first human to be able to control a robot as if it were an extension of the brain. It began with that operation when I was little and . . .

I heard voices outside my room.

My parents.

I quickly saved all I'd written into my diary and rolled out to the common area of our mini-dome to greet them. I knew I had some work ahead of me to convince them I should be able to leave the dome with Rawling. And this time, not through a robot that I controlled.

But as myself.

I was excited—and scared.

CHAPTER 6

"A four-day trip away from the dome? That hasn't been done in the last 10 years. And you're saying Rawling wants to travel two hundred miles?"

This was from my mother, who looked across at my father with concern on her face.

The three of us sat in the center of our mini-dome—Mom and Dad in chairs, and me, of course, in my wheelchair.

Like every other mini-dome, ours had two office-bedrooms with a common living space in the middle. Because we only heated nutri-tubes, we didn't need a kitchen—only a microwave, which hung on the far wall. Another door at the back of the living space led to a small bathroom. It wasn't much. From what I've read about Earth homes, our mini-dome had less space in it than two average bedrooms.

"Rawling says we'll take a platform buggy," I answered. "He'll double up on all the food and oxygen and water just in case anything goes wrong."

Naturally, Mom picked up on the one word a kid should never use when trying to convince his parents of anything.

"Wrong?" Mom repeated, with a quick turn of her head. "What does Rawling think might go wrong?"

As a plant biologist, it was Mom's job to genetically alter Earth plants so they could grow on Mars. Normally she was very businesslike. In fact, until a month ago, when Dad had finally returned from a three-year trip to Earth and back, she'd always been satisfied with a hairstyle that didn't take much fussing and gave her as much time as possible for her science. But now she was letting her hair grow longer and making sure it was done nicely. And that wasn't all. I'd noticed more changes in her. With Dad here to complete our family, she was still every bit a no-nonsense scientist, but she seemed more relaxed and happy.

Except, of course, when her son had just asked permission to leave the safety of the dome for the dangers of the surface of Mars.

Dad coughed. "Assume the worst and hope for the best. That's a great way to plan for travel. I'm sure Rawling is just taking precautions."

"Yes," I said, glad to have someone on my side. Because Dad had been gone so long, he and I had just learned to be friends again.

"So the bigger question," Dad continued, "is why?"

Looking at Dad, for me, was almost like looking in a mirror. If I hadn't been in a wheelchair, people would notice I was growing to be as tall as he was. And we both had dark blond hair.

Because I hadn't said anything, Dad repeated his question.

"Why does Rawling want to take you on a field trip a couple hundred miles away?"

I cleared my throat. "It's so far from the dome, I wouldn't be able to stay connected to the robot if we tried doing it from here. Rawling needs to load the computer and transmitter on the platform buggy and keep it close enough to the robot so that the signal stays strong."

Dad smiled. "Nice try."

"Huh?" I said innocently. He knew me pretty well for someone who had been away from Mars for so long.

"All you did was answer the obvious. What we really want to know is why Rawling wants the robot out there so far from the dome. What does he want it to explore?"

"Oh," I said. "That."

Dad kept smiling. "And . . ."

Rawling had given me permission to tell my parents. But only them. I'd been saving this information for the last.

"Rawling asked me to ask you to keep this to yourselves."

Mom and Dad nodded, so I continued.

"He thinks," I said, "that there may be evidence of an alien civilization." Their reaction was the same that mine had been. Stunned at the thought.

"That's big," Dad said. "Real big."

Mom laughed. "The most staggering discovery in the history of humankind and all you can say is *big?*"

"What would you say?" he asked, grinning back.

She thought for a moment, opened her mouth to say something, changed her mind, and shut it again. Finally she spoke. "It's big. Real big."

"Exactly," he said to her, then turned to me.

"It's so big," Dad said, "that the only way you can go is if I go, too."

CHAPTER 7

That night, as I'd promised Ashley, I went to the dome's telescope. I went early because I loved to spend time alone looking at the Martian night sky.

Earth has an atmosphere that makes the light of the stars twinkle as it moves through air. From Mars, however, it's almost as clear as looking from a spaceship. The lights of the galaxies are like clusters of diamonds, and the powerful dome telescope made the view even more incredible, with millions of tiny bright lights stabbing through the dark of the solar system.

Whenever I sat at the telescope, I reminded myself that I was looking backward through time. Light travels at 186,000 miles per second. So if you were riding in a spaceship that moved at the speed of light, in one minute you'd cover over 11 million miles. In one hour you'd be 670 million miles from your starting point. In one day you'd be over 16 billion miles away. The scary thing about the size of the universe is that the closest star to Earth is more than four light-*years* away, which means you'd have to travel at 186,000 miles per second for nearly 1,500 days to get there. (And some stars are millions of light-years away!)

Why is looking through the telescope like looking backward in time?

If you focus on a star a thousand light-years away, the light that hits your eyes left the star a thousand years ago. It might be in the middle of an explosion as you look at it, but you have no way of knowing for another thousand years until the light of that explosion travels billions and billions and billions of miles to reach you.

In short, the farther you look out into the universe, the farther back in time you can see. To me, that's one of the cool things about astronomy.

I rolled into place at the eyepiece of the telescope, where the dome astronomer usually sat. I punched my password into the computer control pad.

It prompted me for a location. The telescope computer was programmed with 100,000 different locations in the universe, as seen from Mars.

Tonight, however, I wanted to look no farther than the backyard of Mars.

So I entered *Amors asteroids* into the computer.

The electric whine of the telescope motors hummed as the telescope automatically swung into place. But before I was able to lean into the eyepiece, Ashley stepped onto the deck.

"Hey," she said. I heard sadness in her voice. I wondered if it had anything to do with her mom and dad. She hadn't talked about it much, but I knew her parents were divorced. "Whatcha looking for?"

"Asteroids," I said. "More specifically the Amors belt."

Asteroids ranged from the size of a refrigerator to a football stadium to the 15 biggest asteroids, which were each about 150 miles across.

"The Amors belt," she said. "Asteroids in orbit between Mars and Earth."

I grinned. "And the Atens asteroids?"

She paused, beginning to smile because she had a chance to show off her knowledge. "Between Earth and Venus."

"Apollos belt?"

"Much, much more serious. Those are the ones that cross the Earth's orbit."

"Bravo!" I clapped for her.

She bowed as if I were an audience of thousands instead of just a kid in a wheelchair beneath the Martian night. "Any reason you picked asteroids? Usually you get us to look at more exciting things like star explosions. Asteroids are just lumpy rocks that drift like garbage."

"Just thinking about the one that might have hit Mars yesterday. Dad and Rawling figure it was only the size of a spaceship."

I stopped, wondering. Could it actually have been a spaceship? One out of control? Made by an alien civilization? What were we going to find when we finally arrived at the crater that the satellite had photographed?

Dumb, I told myself. *Dumb. Dumb. Dumb.* As if a spaceship had crashed into Mars.

"Doesn't take much, does it?" Ashley said, breaking into my thoughts. "I mean, I was reading up on asteroids today too, and—"

"Ha!" I interrupted. "That's how you knew about the Amors, Atens, and Apollos belts."

She ignored my comment. "And there's a crater in Arizona nearly a mile across, made by an asteroid fragment only half the size of a football field. If one of the bigger asteroids ever hit Mars, it would break the planet in two!"

"Nice thought," I said.

She shrugged. "At least it would take my mind off the news I just got from Earth." The sadness was back in her voice.

"Ashley? Is anything the matter?"

"Well . . ."

Footsteps stopped her from saying anything else.

It was Rawling.

"Hi, guys," he said to us. "Sorry to barge in, but I need to talk to Tyce. It's about our trip. There's no problem if your dad joins us, and we've decided to leave in an hour."

"At night?"

"At night." He didn't give a reason. I thought this was strange. Very strange. Why leave at night?

"So if you could go back down and get ready . . ."

"Um, sure," I said.

Rawling saluted me and spun around, leaving me and Ashley alone again.

"You were saying?" I said to her.

"Nothing," she said. "Where are you going?"

"On a field trip."

"On a field trip! At night? Nobody's gone out in the field since I got here, and nobody's left the dome at night. What's so important?"

"It's just a field trip."

I could see in her eyes that she was hurt I wouldn't tell her. But I couldn't. Worse, I couldn't even tell her why I couldn't tell her.

"Will you be gone long?" she asked.

"I don't know," I said.

"Oh." She seemed to grow small and quiet.

After a few seconds, she reached up and took off one of her silver cross earrings. She handed it to me.

"Keep this," she said.

My face must have looked blank.

"When I'm away from home and in a strange place," she explained, "I like to have a cross to remind me that I don't have to be afraid of anything. Not if I can think of Jesus and of heaven."

I smiled.

"Besides," she said, "you're my only friend under the dome, except for the koalas, and they can't talk. Maybe the cross will also remind you to e-mail me once in a while. I mean, you will have some computers onboard, right?"

I smiled again. "Right," I said. "But there's nothing to worry about." I paused, thinking about our upcoming search. "Really," I said. "Nothing." Almost as if I were trying to convince myself instead of Ashley.

CHAPTER 8

An hour later, we were ready.

Rawling and Dad had loaded all the supplies into a platform buggy, a clear mini-dome perched on a deck that rode on huge rubber tires. Storage compartments and the motor were underneath. The motor didn't burn gasoline because Mars had no oxygen in the atmosphere to allow any fuel to burn. Instead, it ran on electricity made from solar panels that hung off the rear of the platform. The mini-dome looked much like the igloos I've seen in Earth photos. A small tunnel stuck out from the mini-dome onto an open portion of the deck. Then a ladder descended to the ground from there.

From my wheelchair on the ground I had to stretch my head way back to see the platform. Rawling stayed up there as Dad climbed down. Mom was beside me, her hand on my shoulder, as we waited for Dad to get to us.

He kissed Mom's forehead. "I'll miss you. I'm glad I'm only leaving for a few days, not . . ."

He didn't finish his sentence. In a few more weeks, when the planetary orbits were lined up so that the journey from Mars to Earth would be at its shortest, Dad would be on a spaceship again, beginning another three-year journey.

"I'll miss you too." She hugged him. "I'll be praying for you guys."

They kissed again. I coughed and looked the other way.

Mom hugged me and whispered good-bye when they were finished.

"Take care of your dad," she said, speaking more loudly for his benefit.

"Sure," I said. But if I had known what was ahead over the next few days, I might not have sounded so cheerful.

❊

The dome was the quietest it had been all day. Dad and Rawling helped me up the ladder onto the platform deck. Rawling went down again and hauled my wheelchair into the buggy. Bruce, the robot body, was already packed underneath.

This late at night most of the scientists and tekkies were relaxing in their own mini-domes. Because of the quiet, the grinding of the motors that controlled the dome exit seemed louder than usual. The tekkie who was letting us out waved up to us where we sat high above the ground.

"Ready, gentlemen?" Rawling asked as he waved back at the tekkie.

"Ready," I said.

Dad's answer was to move levers, rolling the platform buggy forward into the main dome's igloo tunnel. We moved out of the dome through the inner door and stopped in the short tunnel, which was about twice the length of a platform buggy. The outer door, ahead of us, was still sealed.

The tekkie then closed the inner door behind us, sealing the dome completely. Only then did the tekkie allow the

outer door to open. As the warm, moist, oxygen-filled air followed us out of the dome into the tunnel, it made contact
with the Martian atmosphere. Turning into instant white vapor, it disappeared into the night.

Dad moved the platform buggy forward, and the outer
door shut behind us.

We were on our way to search for alien artifacts.

CHAPTER 9

I wasn't worried about getting lost. The platform buggy, which was running off the stored electricity from the dome's solar panels, held a computer with a global positioning unit (g.p.u.). The g.p.u. tracked our position by satellite and gave us our coordinates on the surface of the planet at all times. Not only that, but as a space pilot, Dad had managed to get to Mars after crossing 50 million miles of space from Earth—like hitting the head of a pin with a bullet from a thousand miles away. So I figured between him and Rawling, a brilliant scientist, that we'd get to the crater, no problem.

"I'm guessing it will take us 14 hours," Rawling said, addressing me. He stood beside Dad at the steering wheel. I sat in my wheelchair to the side, watching through the clear hard plastic of the platform buggy's dome. "It's about two hundred miles. This buggy can do 25 miles an hour, but we'll want to go slower since it's night. Your dad and I will take turns driving."

I nodded at his time estimate. Since gravity on Mars is much different than gravity on Earth, a year on Mars is much longer than on Earth: Mars takes 687 days to circle the sun. But the length of days is similar. Just like Earth, Mars spins, and it takes 24 hours and 37 minutes to complete each rotation.

"I'm hoping," Rawling continued, "that you'll sleep as much as possible. We need you rested, with a sharp concentration level."

"Sure," I said. Rawling had brought onboard the narrow bed with its straps from the computer lab. There were also two small rollout cots for him and Dad. And three space suits with oxygen tanks—one for me in case of emergency, and one for each of them so they could walk around when we got to the site.

I watched the passing landscape in the headlight beams for a few more minutes. While Mars has mountains and extinct volcanoes, there are plenty of valleys, so I was seeing landscape almost like a desert on Earth, except here there were no plants of any kind. Just sand and rocks.

The monstrous tires of the platform buggy rumbled as they pressed against the ground. Because of a good suspension system, the platform deck stayed level most of the time, but there were occasional bumps. I was surprised at how soothing the noise and bumps felt. Maybe it was like being rocked to sleep in a cradle—something I'd only read about.

But I wasn't ready to sleep. Not yet.

I asked Rawling the question I'd been saving. "Why did we have to leave tonight in such a big rush?"

"Politics," Rawling answered. "Plain and simple."

Dad kept his eye on the white circles of light cast by the headlight beams.

Rawling gave his attention to me. "Think of what it would mean on Earth if we discovered evidence of an alien civilization. If those black boxes came from beings who once lived on Mars or from beings from another solar system who left them on Mars, this would be the greatest discovery in the history of humankind."

"With our names all over it, right?" I grinned. "We'd be known forever!"

Dad took his eyes off the headlight beams briefly and snorted. "My son, the space explorer." He smiled, shook his head with affection, and kept driving.

"For starters," Rawling explained to me, "if what we find belonged to an ancient Martian civilization, we might be able to learn a tremendous amount about how to recolonize the planet. Did they live underground? Where did they get power? How did they make food? All those answers will be extremely valuable."

"And if these black boxes aren't from a Martian civilization . . ."

"Since no other planets other than Mars and Earth are potentially inhabitable, it means the boxes had to come from outside the solar system. Which would be far more incredible."

"An alien is an alien," I pointed out. "No matter where it's from."

"Not quite," Rawling said. "Aliens from outside this solar system could only get here with some type of transportation that overcomes the tremendous distances. Think about it. With the best technology we have, it still takes three years to catch an orbit to take us from Mars to Earth and back. Imagine being able to travel to the stars."

"Close to light speed travel!" Dad said. Now, as a space pilot, he was very interested.

"That's a big stretch to conclude from the presence of unexplained black boxes," Rawling cautioned. "But a possible stretch."

"Well," I said, "what does this have to do with politics and the reason we left in such a hurry?"

"If we find evidence of an alien civilization, scientists will be extremely curious to learn from it. And the Earth government will also want to know if it needs to defend the Earth against future alien invasions. Given these two factors, how much money do you think the United Nations' Science Agency would be prepared to spend on the Mars Project?"

Even I understood that kind of politics. "Tons and tons and tons," I answered.

Rawling nodded. "Right now, it's costing Earth about $200 billion a year to support the dome. You can bet that money would be doubled or tripled. Or more."

He paused as the platform buggy hit a big bump. Rawling waited for the platform to level itself and stop shaking.

"Here's why we couldn't wait until tomorrow to leave. Travel to the crater and back will take up to two days altogether. I'd like at least two days to explore and learn what we can. That gives us four days. Even with that, we'll barely make the deadline."

"Deadline for what?"

"In four days," Rawling told me, "the United Nations is voting on budget issues. Specifically, the amount of money they are going to commit to the Mars Project. We need to find out about this by then, or else."

I asked the obvious. "Or else what?"

"It's not public knowledge," Rawling said. "But after all these years and with progress so slow, there are some people on Earth who wonder if the government should be spending $200 billion a year on the dome. When we first left for Mars 15 years ago, we knew that the issue of funding would come up at the end of the 15th year. Now that time is here. As director, I've found out there's a good chance they're going to cut the budget in half at that meeting. Or more. Which will mean the end of the dome as we know it." Rawling let out a deep breath. "In other words, finding evidence of aliens will ensure that all of us stay on Mars."

CHAPTER 10

Rawling wanted me to get as much sleep as possible. He had already dimmed the interior lights. Now he shut them off completely so that only the instrument panels glowed.

I lay on my narrow bed, staring through the clear hard plastic of the platform dome.

The stars were crisp diamond points against the black velvet of the Martian night. And although Mars does have a moon—in fact, two—neither moon gives much light. They are like giant potatoes—huge lumps of rock, each less than 20 miles across.

As I stared upward, waiting to get tired enough to sleep, I was able to see a solar system sight so beautiful that I felt sorry for people on Earth, because they'll never be able to see it. Not unless they actually leave Earth.

What I saw was a round white-and-blue ball hanging against the eternal darkness. The Earth itself. With a telescope from Mars, you can see the swirls of cloud cover and watch hurricanes develop. From the platform buggy, however, I had to rely on my memory of telescope sighting.

How incredible, the Earth. The atmosphere that surrounds it is microscopic compared to the size of the planet.

Yet this thin fabric of nitrogen and oxygen makes life possible. Without atmosphere, there's no water, no conservation of heat.

The angle of the tilt of the Earth is perfectly suited to give seasons. The size is perfect too. Bigger planets like Venus have too many volcanoes and erupt so much carbon dioxide that the greenhouse effect heats them to 850 degrees Fahrenheit. Smaller planets like Mercury can't hold their atmosphere.

And Earth's moon? Planets without a large moon flip-flop on the axis of rotation, literally throwing the planet back and forth, making it impossible for life to survive climate changes.

If the Earth were only one percent closer to the sun (think of taking only one penny off a stack of one hundred pennies), it would get too hot. Only 5 percent farther away, and it would freeze, like Mars. If the Earth didn't have a nearly perfect circular orbit—always 93 million miles away—it would get too close to and too far from the sun.

In other words, life on Earth only exists because the planet is the right size, always at the right distance from the right-sized sun, with the right-sized moon circling it at the right distance.

All of this has convinced me that the Earth was created for a reason. And that someone—a powerful Someone, God—made it that way so life could exist. After years of finding it hard to believe in him, I'd been thinking a lot about him over the past month. It had all started with the oxygen crisis and wondering what would happen to me if I died.

I started getting drowsier as these thoughts went through my mind.

Then Ashley's question popped back into my thoughts. *Why is there something instead of nothing? And what was here instead of the universe before the nothing be-came something? How can time start? Did it start when the universe started? Or is time forever?*

I closed my eyes against the stars above and let all these questions run through my mind again and again and again.

It must have looked like I was asleep because Rawling and my dad started talking softly.

"It's a big responsibility," Rawling said. "I'm sorry I have to throw it on Tyce's shoulders."

That worried me. What exactly was going to be so diffi-cult?

"It has to be done," Dad answered just as softly. "But if anyone can do it, it's Tyce. Words can't tell you how proud I am to have him as a son."

A month ago, he hardly felt like a father to me. Now it was different. Hearing him say that made me happy.

I fell asleep with a smile on my face.

And I woke up to a loud screeching noise.

CHAPTER 11

The screeching sound was followed by a big jolt of the platform buggy.

In bed, I struggled to sit up. I leaned on my elbows and blinked myself completely awake. The first rays of sun had reached across the horizon, showing the jagged edges of ancient rust-red volcanoes on all sides of us.

"Tyce," Dad said from behind the controls, "you can relax. We're fine."

Rawling was at the side of the platform, peering downward through the clear protective plastic. "I'm not sure about one of our tires though."

The platform deck had begun to tilt in Rawling's direction.

"Some of this lava is sharp as a razor," Rawling continued. "I think it cut one of the rear tires."

Dad leaned back in his chair and rubbed his face. It looked like he'd been at the controls the entire time I'd slept.

"We've got a compressor underneath," Rawling said. "All we need to do is plug the leak with a repair kit, and we'll be on our way."

I remembered the tires were filled with carbon dioxide so we could pump into them straight from the atmosphere.

Dad stood and stretched. "Flip a coin to see who goes out there?"

"Nope," Rawling said. He pointed at me. "Here's where you get to see how good your son is."

❉

"Run through the checklist," Rawling told me as he tightened straps across my legs to hold me to the bed. If I moved, the connection between the antenna plug in my spine and the computer receiver on the other side of the platform deck could be broken.

"First," I said, "no robot contact with any electrical sources. Ever." Because my spinal nerves were attached to the antenna plug, any electrical current going into or through the robot could seriously damage the neurons of my brain. It had happened once—a slight shock—and I'd been out for 6 minutes and 10 seconds.

"Check." We did this every time. Rawling insisted on it. He said on Earth, airline pilots did the same thing before every flight because safety was so important.

Rawling pulled the straps down across my stomach and chest as I continued. "Second, I disengage instantly at the first warning of any damage to the robot's computer drive." My brain circuits worked so closely with the computer circuits during the linkup that harm to the computer could spill over and harm my brain.

"Check." Rawling strapped my head into position.

"How does he disengage?" Dad asked. This was the first time he'd actually seen me at work, though he had unstrapped me once when Rawling was called away. Dad knew, of course, the theory behind it, but whenever I'd gone on practice runs, he'd been unable to get away from his own work.

"I shout *Stop!* in my mind," I said. "Sounds strange, but that's all it takes. My brain controls the virtual-reality controls no differently than it controls my hand muscles or arm muscles."

There's a short, dark rod, hardly thicker than a needle, wedged directly into my spinal column, at the bottom of my neck, just above the top of my shoulder blades. From that rod, thousands of tiny biological implants—they look like hairs—stick out of the end of the needle into the middle of my spinal column. Each of the fibers, which have grown into my nerves, has a core that transmits tiny impulses of electricity, allowing my brain to control a robot's computer.

This was part of the long-term plan to develop Mars: to use robots to explore the planet. Humans need oxygen and water and heat to survive on the surface. Robots don't. But robots can't think like humans. From all my years of training with a computer simulation program, my mind knows all the muscle moves it takes to handle the virtual-reality controls. Handling the robot is no different, except instead of actually moving my muscles, I imagine I'm moving the muscles. My brain then sends the proper nerve impulses to the robot, and it moves the way I make the robot move in the virtual-reality computer program.

I admit, it is cool. Almost worth being in a wheelchair. After all, the experimental operation is what caused my legs to be useless.

"Any last questions?" Rawling asked me. "We'll communicate by radio, and I'll direct you on the technical aspects of fixing the tire."

"No questions," I said.

Rawling placed a blindfold over my eyes.

In the darkness that now covered me, I spoke to my dad. "Don't worry. I like this. A lot."

Bruce, the robot, was a freedom that made up for having legs that don't work. No one else could wander the planet like I could.

"Headset?" Rawling asked.

"Headset," I confirmed.

He placed a soundproof headset on my ears. The fewer distractions to reach my brain in my real body, the better.

It was dark and silent then, while I waited. I knew Rawling needed to make some computer entries. The antenna plug on my back transmitted and received signals on an invisible X-ray frequency to the computer, which in turn relayed signals to and from the robot body. In my mind, there was no difference between handling the robot and handling a virtual-reality program like any kid on Earth. Except for the fact that the X-ray frequency for the robot had a range of 20 miles. Like a remote control that could penetrate walls and rock and anything that might get between the computer here and the robot body.

I'd trained in virtual-reality simulations ever since I was eight, so handling the robot body was like handling my own body.

Blindfolded and in the silence of the headset, I waited for a sensation that had become familiar and beautiful for me. The sensation of entering the robot computer.

My wait wasn't long.

In the darkness and silence, I began to fall off a high, invisible cliff into a deep, invisible hole.

I kept falling and falling and falling. . . .

CHAPTER 12

Directly beneath the platform deck, the robot's four video lenses opened. Light patterns were translated digitally and became electrical impulses that followed the electronic circuitry into the computer drive of the robot. From there, they were translated into X-ray waves that traveled to the receiver above. The receiver then beamed to the wires of my jumpsuit, which were connected to the antenna plug in my spine. The electrical impulses moved instantly up the nerves of my spinal column into my brain, where my brain did what it always did when light entered my real eyes and hit the optical nerves that reached into my brain—it translated the light patterns into images.

Although the lenses didn't blink, in my mind, it felt like I blinked into focus.

The monstrous tires of the platform buggy filled most of my view. I saw the lightweight titanium and graphite support beams of the underside of the platform.

The sound of wind and sand drifting across sand reached the robot's intake speakers and translated into sound in my mind.

I thought about moving the robot arms. And, instantly, it

happened. I brought both titanium hands up in front of a video lens and flexed the robot's fingers, wiggling them to make sure everything worked properly.

Everything did.

The robot body hung in a suspended cage. I pushed the button that lowered it. When the cage gently rested on the ground, I pushed another button that opened the door.

I rolled out the robot onto the surface of Mars. The platform buggy was like a giant wagon above me, so I moved away, out from under the wheels and storage compartments, far enough to be able to see the entire mini-dome.

I waved upward at Rawling and Dad, who were looking for me.

It was weird, seeing them wave back down while only a few feet from them my actual body was motionless on the bed.

I knew how the robot body looked to them.

The lower body is much like my wheelchair. Except that instead of a pair of legs, there is an axle that connects two wheels. The robot's upper body is merely a short, thick, hollow pole that sticks through the axle, with a heavy weight to counterbalance the arms and head. Within this weight is the battery that powers the robot, with wires running up inside the hollow pole.

The upper end of the pole has a crosspiece to which arms are attached. They are able to swing freely without hitting the wheels. Like the rest of the robot, they are made of titanium and jointed like human arms, with one difference. All the joints swivel. The hands, too, are like human hands, but with only three fingers and a thumb instead of four fingers and a thumb.

Four video lenses at the top of the pole serve as eyes. One faces forward, one backward, and one to each side.

Three tiny speakers, attached to the underside of the video lenses, play the role of ears, taking sound in. The fourth speaker, on the underside of the video lens that faces forward, produces sound and allows me to make my voice heard.

The computer drive of the robot is well protected within the hollow titanium pole that serves as the robot's upper body. Since it is mounted on shock absorbers, the robot can fall 10 feet without shaking the computer drive. This computer drive has a short antenna plug-in at the back of the pole to give and take X-ray signals.

The robot is amazing. It has heat sensors that detect infrared, so I can see in total darkness. The video lenses' telescoping is powerful enough that I can recognize a person's face from five miles away. But I can zoom in close on something nearby and look at it as if using a microscope.

I can amplify hearing and pick up sounds at higher and lower levels than human hearing. The fibers wired into the titanium let me feel dust falling, if I want to concentrate on that minute of a level. The fibers also let me speak easily, just as if I were using a microphone.

The robot can't smell or taste, however. But one of the fingers is wired to perform material testing. All I need are a few specks of the material, and this finger will heat up, burn the material, and analyze the contents.

The robot is strong, too. The titanium hands can grip a steel bar and bend it.

Did I mention it's fast? Its wheels will move three times faster than any human can sprint. But this morning, I had nowhere to go. My job was very simple. Fix a tire.

Rawling had placed a communications radio just outside the dome of the platform buggy. I saw him lift his radio to his mouth. Instantly, my radio speaker rumbled with his voice.

"Tyce, check the tire to see if the leak is obvious."

I rolled over to the collapsed tire. I scanned it with my video lens.

"Nothing unusual," I reported in my robot voice. "Can you slowly roll the platform buggy ahead?"

Moments later, it rolled forward in a lopsided way.

Immediately, as the part of the tire that had been resting on the ground came into view, I saw the reason for the screeching sound.

As Rawling had guessed, a long narrow piece of lava rock stuck from the tire. In fact, it stuck out so far that it scraped the underside of the platform deck each time the tire rolled over.

"Got it!" I said.

I explained what I saw.

With lots of instruction from Rawling, the strong robot hands and arms, and all the right equipment, I was able to seal the leak and refill the tire with compressed carbon dioxide.

It was a simple, routine piece of work.

The only unusual thing about it was a small gray box. I noticed it was attached to the axle of the wheel. I wondered if it was part of the g.p.u., because it had some wires sticking out, like communications antennas.

I loaded the robot body in the cage and raised the cage off the ground so the robot would hang and swing in safety. Then I gave the stop command to disengage from the computer program that controlled the robot.

From the bed inside the platform buggy's mini-dome, I calmly told Rawling I was ready to be unstrapped.

Seconds later, someone took off my headset and my blindfold.

It wasn't Rawling. It was Dad.

Rawling was at the base radio. Talking.

And when I heard what he said, I forgot all about that small gray plastic box beneath the platform deck.

CHAPTER 13

"Blaine Steven has taken control of the dome?" I heard Rawling say, disbelief in his voice. "He has no authority to do that!"

Blaine Steven? Ex-director? But he was under guard until the next spaceship left Mars to take him to Earth.

"Sir," the communications tekkie said, "half an hour ago, we received a transmission from Earth. It has the proper electronic identification code that identifies it as a Science Agency message. It granted Blaine Steven full directorship in your absence. It—"

Sudden silence.

"Platform one to main base," Rawling said, trying to get the communications tekkie back. "Platform one to main base."

"Dr. McTigre." The sound of the radio communications was tinny, but I still recognized the new voice. Blaine Steven. He'd lost his position over a month ago because of how he'd mishandled an oxygen level zero situation that nearly killed 180 people under the dome. And now he was back?

"This is Rawling." There was controlled anger in his voice.

"And this is Director Blaine Steven. Our computer shows your position clearly. Please explain to me what you are doing so far from base."

Rawling opened and closed his mouth several times.

"That is an order, Dr. McTigre."

I thought I understood Rawling's confusion. If it was true that the Science Agency had reinstated Blaine Steven as director, Rawling had no choice. The director of the dome was like a five-star general in the military. But could Rawling believe the Science Agency had given Blaine Steven the authority?

"That is an order, Dr. McTigre. If you do not respond, I will consider this mutiny."

Mutiny. The worst possible offense under the dome. With penalties so severe that the person would not only be sent back to Earth, but also placed in prison for life.

Rawling shook his head at us and frowned. Then he sighed and said into the radio microphone, "I would rather not explain over the airwaves. However, if you check the logbook on my computer, you will see the urgency of this situation."

Blaine Steven's voice became less harsh. "You're a good man, McTigre. I know you wouldn't be out there without good reason. I will review the logbook. In the meantime, continue with your mission unless you receive a direct order from me to return. I am in control now and will not permit unauthorized field trips. Understood?"

Rawling's jaw clenched with anger. "Understood."

"And I want reports every six hours. Understood?" Steven demanded.

"Understood."

"Good-bye." Blaine Steven clicked off without even waiting for Rawling to say good-bye.

Rawling slowly hung up the radio microphone. "This doesn't make sense," he said, lifting his eyes first to Dad's, then to mine. "No sense at all."

CHAPTER 14

I stood at the edge of the crater in the robot body. Below were boulders and rocks, darker red than most Martian rocks because they'd been so recently exposed to the surface by the explosion that had caused the crater.

About 12 miles away, a mountain range filled my view, almost bright red with late-afternoon sun. The temperature was warm for Mars, about 40 degrees Fahrenheit, and just a little windy.

Behind me, towering above Bruce's titanium shell, was the platform buggy. It threw long shadows across the robot body and into the crater. We'd traveled most of the rest of the day, because repairing the tire had delayed our arrival here. Now the sun was only two hours away from setting.

To begin, Rawling had given me a simple assignment. All he needed was a quick survey. With night coming so soon, he didn't think we'd be able to get much else done.

A thin metal cable was attached to the frame of the platform buggy. This cable dangled over the edge of the crater and all the way to the bottom. Just like in my earlier practice run of cliff climbing when I was carrying the crash-test dummy, I held grippers in each hand, ready to clamp the wire as I let myself down to the bottom of the crater.

Five large, black boxes were centered down there among the boulders and rocks.

Had an ancient Martian civilization left them behind?

Had aliens from outside the solar system hidden them there?

What was inside those mysterious boxes?

It was my job to find out.

⚛

Slowly I climbed down the cable hand by hand. The wheels of my robot body moved easily, and the entire descent went without any trouble.

Ten minutes later I was on the floor of the crater.

It was almost like being in a maze.

The boulders were large enough that I couldn't see over the top of them. In many places, they were so close together that I couldn't roll between them. I was forced to backtrack and look for other ways around them.

It had been easy enough to see the large, black boxes from above. They formed the center of a large ring of the boulders, as if the explosion had left them there and thrown the rocks and boulders outward. So seeing the center of the crater from above had been easy.

Down here, though, with the rough, rust-colored rock of the boulders blocking my view in every direction, it was more difficult.

It took 10 more minutes of wandering around the huge boulders until I finally arrived at the opening of the center of the crater.

I got my first close look at the black boxes. Was it the first time a human had seen them?

As I rolled the robot body toward them, I was confident Dad and Rawling were seeing them, too, through the video lenses that also served as the robot's eyes. They recorded everything on a monitor that Dad and Rawling could watch as I moved around.

They, however, could only watch.

Because I could control the robot body as if I were in a virtual-reality computer game, I could do much more. Like get so close that the huge black boxes surrounded me like a prison wall.

Close up, the black of the sides of the boxes was dull. Not dull like weathered paint, but a black that seemed to soak up light.

I tapped the side of the nearest box. I don't know what I was expecting. To hear if it was hollow, perhaps.

I did not, however, expect the box to start moving.

Which it did. If the robot body had had a heart, it would have stopped in shock. Because silently the box seemed to split at the corner nearest me. And slowly, very slowly, the sides of the box began to separate.

CHAPTER 15

I scooted backwards, letting my video lens roam up and down as the split in the box grew wider and wider.

Down here the crater was filled with shadows because of the angle of the sun. It was difficult to see inside the black box as it opened.

I was ready for anything.

Would an alien charge out at me, awakened from hundreds or thousands of centuries of hibernation?

Would a preprogrammed robot appear with instructions?

Had I triggered a three-dimensional hologram to speak to me?

Would there be something so totally beyond human culture that I wouldn't be able to understand what I was seeing?

The sides slowly continued to open. Still I saw nothing but blackness in the interior of the box.

I wasn't worried about my own safety. I was in the robot body. All I had to do was shout *Stop!* in my mind, and I'd instantly disengage from controlling the robot. If anything harmed the robot body, which would be difficult to do anyway, my brain and my own body would still be safe in the platform buggy.

Finally, the box stopped all movement.

I waited.

Nothing happened.

I rolled closer again. Cautiously.

Nothing happened.

Still closer.

The inside of the box seemed to soak up all light. In the shadows of the crater, it was like looking into an infinitely deep cave.

Still closer. I stopped about 20 feet from the open black box.

Then I saw it, floating in the air. In the exact center of the box. It was a round object the size of a human head.

I knew what Rawling would want me to do at this point: zoom in closer with my video lens and record the object for him and Dad to examine on the monitor.

I focused closer and opened the video lens as wide as possible to capture as much light as it could.

That's when I saw the object was not a head. It was more like a gyroscope globe—a wheel or disk that spins rapidly around an axis—and made of thin, curved, shiny tubing. It rotated slowly. But the weirdest part was that it just hung there, in the center of the box, like it was defying gravity.

That's all that I could see inside this huge, black box.

I had my instructions from Rawling. "Just observe and record," he'd said firmly. "Disengage at the first sign of danger. Let the video lenses do the work. Do not interfere with anything."

I had to know, however. Was that rotating globe hanging from something?

I wondered about waiting until I'd discussed it with Rawling. But what if the black box closed? What if exposure to the Martian atmosphere damaged it?

I decided to get as close as possible.

I rolled forward until I was almost at the black box.

The gleaming globe hung there, like a silent eye staring back at me.

I saw that it rotated from left to right, then up and down, then right to left, then down and up.

How could it rotate in so many different directions if it was hanging from something like a black wire hidden in the darkness of the box?

But if nothing was holding it, how could it hang there against the force of gravity?

I wasn't going to touch the globe. No, I had Rawling's instructions. All I wanted to do was pass the titanium hand of the robot body over the top of the suspended globe. I wanted to see if somehow something was holding it in place.

So I carefully reached into the box.

And my entire world exploded.

CHAPTER 16

I woke to darkness.

Not the darkness of the blindfold that covered my own eyes.

But to the darkness of the Martian night, with the pinpoints of light—the stars—coming through the clear plastic of the platform buggy's mini-dome.

"Hello?" I croaked. "Hello?"

I heard the sound of footsteps as Rawling and Dad both rushed toward me.

"Tyce!" Dad said. I heard the worry in his voice.

"Tyce!" Rawling said, a millisecond later.

The loudness of both their voices struck like a sledgehammer to the side of my head.

"Whisper," I pleaded. "Just whisper."

A tiny light appeared in Rawling's hand. "I want to check your pupils," he said. He beamed the light in my eye. "Better. Much better."

"It was worse?" I asked, as I lay on the bed with Dad and Rawling now beside me.

"Somehow a massive electrical current short-circuited

the robot computer drive. For you, it was the equivalent of running your head into a wall."

"Felt like it," I said, groaning.

"How's everything else?" Rawling asked. "Fingers, hands, arms. Start moving."

I sat up carefully.

"Oh, no!" I cried.

"What?" Dad asked. "What is it?"

"My legs! I can't move them!" I stopped, pausing dramatically. "Forgot. I couldn't move them before either."

"Very funny," Dad growled. "Very, very funny."

I thought it was. I mean, if I couldn't joke about being in a wheelchair, then it meant I was feeling too sorry for myself. I'd learned to accept it a long time ago.

Dad helped me into my wheelchair.

Rawling had moved to the platform buggy controls. He turned up the interior lights. "Let's talk," he said, pulling up a chair beside me.

Dad did the same so that we formed a small semicircle.

"We have everything on video until you reached inside," Rawling continued. "Then the short-circuit cut everything out. I thought you'd promised not to touch or interfere with anything you saw."

I nodded. I explained that all I'd wanted to do was see if the thing was floating. I hadn't intended to touch anything at all.

"Maybe there was some kind of protective force field," I said.

"Maybe," Rawling said. "But we won't find out until tomorrow. Your dad's going to go down there in a protective suit and pull the robot body away from the black boxes. Hopefully all he'll need to do is replace a circuit breaker in the computer hard drive and Bruce will be ready again. But we can't have you knocking yourself out. No damage was done this time, but next time . . ."

Rawling didn't need to finish his statement.

"What do you think that globe was?" I asked. We were still speaking in low voices. Not only was it easier on my headache, but it seemed to fit. After all, we were two hundred miles away from the main dome, sheltered from the Martian night only by a thin layer of plastic that held in the warmth and oxygen we needed to live. We were alone and isolated, in the dark, only a stone's throw from a mysterious set of objects that might have been left in the crater by aliens.

"We've reviewed the videos again and again," Dad said. "We're afraid to let ourselves believe what we think it is. Rawling doesn't want to send a satellite feed of the video to the main dome yet, even though Blaine Steven has gone from asking for reports every six hours to calling us every hour. Because if it's what we think it is . . ."

Rawling let out a deep breath. "You see, Tyce, we have no idea how long those black boxes have been buried. No idea how long that globe has been spinning and spinning. For all we know, it's been there for thousands of years, waiting for someone to discover it."

"Have you heard of a perpetual motion machine?" Dad asked me.

"I've heard about people trying to find a way to make one," I said. "It's a machine that never loses energy. It'll stay in motion forever."

"Right," he said. "Inventors on Earth have been trying to come up with one for centuries. Tell me. Why is it impossible to make one?"

"Easy," I said. "Friction. No matter how efficient a machine is, it will lose energy as it fights friction. The moving parts inside cause friction. Air outside causes friction. Contact with the ground will cause friction."

"What if the machine has some force that actually allows it to act against gravity?" Dad asked. "Then what?"

"Antigravity. That's as impossible as perpetual motion." Neither replied.

"No way," I said. "You think this thing has both? Antigravity *and* some energy source to allow perpetual motion?"

"How else can you explain it?" Rawling said, scratching his head in thought. "We've run the video in slow motion and reviewed it dozens of times. This *thing* has no apparent source of power and nothing to hold it in place. Yet we can't guess how long it's been spinning against gravity."

"Wow," I said. "It must be alien."

"That fact alone would be staggering beyond belief," Dad said. "But if somehow mankind could understand how to make an antigravity force, it would change our history forever. We could put buildings together that don't need support. Transporting goods would be cheap. People might travel in the air as easily as walking across a street. Add on top of that a way to keep a machine in motion without losing energy, and . . ."

Rawling shook his head in awe. "If that's truly what it is, I don't think we can comprehend how much this means to the human race."

CHAPTER 17

I don't think we can comprehend how much this means to the human race.

As I tried to sleep, Rawling's words echoed again and again in my mind.

Antigravity? Without gravity to cause friction, cars and trains would move with no more than the push of a fingertip. Airplanes would be weightless. It would change all types of transportation so that fuel would barely be needed. And what if small antigravity devices were made so that people could float? Wow!

Perpetual motion? If scientists could figure out what made that globe revolve, they might be able to apply the principle to large motors. What would the Earth be like without fights over energy?

The whole purpose of the Mars colony was to help the overpopulated world. It was expected to take one hundred years or more. In that time, millions of people might die from starvation or war.

And now?

Just maybe, machines with antigravity or perpetual

motion motors might solve the problems. Lives would be saved. Earth would be saved.

Thinking about all this, I couldn't sleep.

I twisted and turned in my bed.

I saw that Dad was sitting near the side of the platform, staring through the clear plastic at the dark, still Martian landscape.

"Dad?" I whispered.

"Yes, Tyce," he whispered back.

"You can't sleep either?"

He laughed softly. "Just thinking."

"Me too," I said.

Dad stood. He rolled my wheelchair toward me and stopped it near the bed. He sat in it, facing me.

"Thinking about what?"

"How what we've discovered might solve so many problems for humans."

Dad was quiet for so long, I wondered if he'd heard me.

He sighed. "A lot of people will think that. But they'll be wrong."

"Wrong?" I asked. I propped myself up on my elbows. Above me, the stars were intense against the black Martian sky.

"It's sad and funny," he answered. "For as long as there have been people, we humans have always looked for ways to make the perfect society. And we've always failed. People think the next solution will work, but it never does."

"The perfect society?"

"Everybody happy. No wars, no crime. Enough property and resources shared so that people aren't greedy or hateful. For the last four centuries, science has tried to accomplish that. Better medicine. Better computers. Better psychiatry. And on and on and on. But nothing works."

"Antigravity," I protested. "Machines that conserve energy forever. Now people won't need to fight or steal, right?"

"Wrong. You know we've had talks about this. Humans have souls, Tyce. We're empty without God to fill us. We keep looking for other solutions because we don't want to admit the need."

He laughed again. "So people on Earth are going to hear about this and think we've been saved. By aliens. They're going to be more willing to believe in aliens than in God. But I'll tell you what. They can have all the money, power, resources in the world, and they'll still feel like they're missing something. Antigravity machines or perpetual motion machines aren't the answer. Accepting Jesus, God's Son, into your heart so you can be at peace with God is."

I thought that over. "That's why you and Mom aren't afraid, isn't it?"

"It's a matter of perspective, Tyce. Once you accept that God loves you—in fact, so much he gave his Son's life for you—you can begin to look beyond the everyday worries. If you choose to believe in Jesus, you don't have to worry about where your soul will go when you die. You'll be in heaven, with God."

I ran my fingers over Ashley's silver cross earring, which hung on the chain around my neck. Things were beginning to make more sense.

After all, Jesus, who'd walked on Earth, had come to give that same message. He'd claimed to be God and told people to trust in him. To trust in his message that they could be saved from death and live with God forever. That they could have purpose and meaning in their lives if they gave their lives to him. There was a lot of peace in that.

"Tyce?"

I guess I'd been quiet for a few minutes.

"Dad?"

We were still whispering.

"That make sense to you?"

I smiled in the darkness.

"Yeah," I said. "It does."

CHAPTER 18

"Done?" Rawling said into the handheld communication device.

"Done." It was my dad's voice. He was in the crater, in his space suit, with a handheld, too. "Your guess was correct, Rawling. All it took was a fuse."

A few minutes earlier, Dad had reported finding the robot body frozen in place a few paces back from the mysterious black box, which he'd found closed.

"Good," Rawling answered. "Box still closed?"

"Still closed." There was a pause. "It's opening again. All I did was tap it, just like Tyce did yesterday."

"Good again. And the antigravity gyroscope globe?"

"Hang on. The door's still opening. It's . . . it's . . . yes. It's still there."

"I'll send Tyce right down," Rawling said.

He nodded in my direction. I was already on the bed, my legs strapped into place. I'd been awake since dawn, waiting for this chance.

Rawling stepped over to the bed. We went through the regular checklist as he got me ready.

"The other boxes are opening too," Dad said into his handheld.

Now I was on my back, blindfold over my eyes.

"I can't believe this," Dad said. "I just can't believe this! Get Tyce here as fast as you can!"

Rawling slipped the headset over my ears.

Ten seconds later, I began that deep fall into deep black.

※

Light entered the robot body's video lenses.

I scanned four directions. The boulders were behind me, with one black box open directly in front of them. The gyroscope globe still floated and rotated in its eerie, awesome way.

I knew better than to try to reach inside that black box.

"Dad?" I said through the robot voice speaker. "Dad?"

"Over here, Tyce!" His voice was muffled coming out of his space helmet. "Get ready to record all this!"

Dad was around the corner of the black box open in front of me. In his space suit, he looked like a marshmallow man. He pointed at the inside of the box as I rolled into his sight.

The edges of the box threw dark, crisp shadows on the rocky soil. But I didn't spend much time admiring the blue of the sun or the butterscotch of the sky.

Not with what caught my eye.

Aliens!

Human-sized aliens! Frozen in position. Two of them.

They were like giant ants. Six arms, and a two-sectioned body instead of three. Instead of an antlike head, however, each had a smooth, egg-shaped face. Their eyes were black. Two, like a human, but easily five times the size of human eyes, and on the bottom of the face. Black, gaping holes were open wide on their foreheads.

None wore clothing or anything that I recognized as clothing.

Instead, each was coated with a layer of thick, clear plastic. The material might not have been plastic, but that's the only way I could describe it.

Their arms were tucked against their sides. I wondered if they were alive.

"Hibernation?" I asked Dad. The words barely came out of my mouth because I was hardly able to breathe. "Or dead and buried like this?"

"I don't know," Dad said. "All the other boxes are identical. Two per box. Except for the one box you opened yesterday. That holds the antigravity gyroscope globe."

I scanned the inside of the box with the robot's video lenses, trusting all this was showing up on Rawling's monitor back on the platform buggy.

I went from box to box, doing the same with each. Dad was right. There were two aliens per box, each about the same size.

I wondered what had happened. Maybe they'd allowed themselves to be sealed, expecting that someday other aliens would come back and revive them.

Or maybe they'd been killed and thrown into the boxes, like prisoners of some intergalactic war.

Or maybe they were old and had died of natural causes, and the clear plastic coating was the alien way of mummifying them.

Or maybe . . .

"Tyce!"

Dad was shouting in panic.

I reversed the robot and sped as fast as I could in the direction of his voice.

I reached Dad quickly and stared at the inside of the box he pointed at. The alien forms were beginning to melt down, as if an invisible fire had taken hold of them.

And five seconds later, the box itself exploded, knocking me backwards and slamming me into a boulder.

As the robot body wobbled back into balance, a second box exploded.

Then a third. And a fourth. And a fifth.

After that, the ground began to slide into itself, as if it were water in slow motion, going down a drain.

"Dad!" I shouted. "Dad!"

CHAPTER 19

I wheeled in tight circles until I found him.

The blast had thrown him against a boulder. His eyes were closed, and he was slumped and limp. His space helmet was cracked, and blood trickled from the corner of his mouth.

Since everyone at the dome is required to take first aid, I knew one of the first rules was not to move the injured person. But that only applied if the person wasn't in further danger where he was.

In this case, with the ground slipping away, I had to move Dad quickly.

I knew his space helmet was fine, for now. If the crack had gone all the way through, I'd be seeing a hiss of vapor as the moist oxygen-filled air of his space suit leaked away, along with his life.

I didn't know about his back. He could have broken it. Under ideal circumstances, two men would carefully place him on a stretcher board and strap him so he was immobile.

These were not ideal circumstances.

Whatever booby trap the aliens had left, it was working quickly.

It felt like a hole had opened beneath the circle where the black boxes had been. The hole was sucking sand and small rocks downward.

With the robot's titanium arms, I lifted Dad as gently as I could.

I spun a tight circle, grateful that the robot had strength I'd never hope to get in my own body.

The cable hung over the edge of the crater. Earlier, when Dad had gone into the crater to fix the robot's computer drive, he'd climbed down alone, using the grippers. Now the robot would have to carry him.

I raced to the cable, fighting the moving rivers of sand that tried to pull me down into the hole.

Only then did I realize how much trouble this would be.

I couldn't strap Dad to my back. In the practice runs, Rawling and I had assumed that any passengers would strap themselves into place.

Dad was unconscious.

And the sand began to suck at my robot wheels.

In my mind, I shouted *Stop!* to disengage myself from the robot controls.

⚛

I woke up in the platform buggy.

"Rawling," I said into the darkness and the silence. I was blindfolded and in the headset, so I had to trust he'd listen. "You've seen what happened on the monitors. I need to get Dad back up. But I can't without your help. Back the platform buggy away from the edge of the crater. Now!"

With time running out for Dad, I was glad Rawling had made me go on so many practice runs. I knew how to slip back into the virtual reality of the robot controls without his coaching.

Into the darkness, I began to fall. . . .

※

Light entered the robot's video lenses.

Straight ahead were the red rock walls of the crater.

The cable dangled in front.

And in the robot's arms was my dad's quiet body.

I grabbed the cable with a gripper clamp in the robot's right hand and held Dad firmly in the left arm.

I braced myself, hoping Rawling understood what I needed.

Seconds later, sand disappeared from under me.

Because I was hanging on to the cable, I didn't roll backwards with the sand.

Soon after that, the cable lurched upward as Rawling eased the platform buggy away from the crater.

I held on, letting him tow the robot body and Dad up the crater wall. The robot wheels rolled smoothly.

I kept a good grip on Dad and rode the cable all the way up the wall until, finally, the cable towed me over the edge and onto the safe, flat ground.

Instantly I released the cable and raced toward the platform buggy.

When I got there, Rawling was already in a space suit and climbing down to help me with Dad.

CHAPTER 20

"All I've got is a doozy of a headache," Dad said. His grin was weak, and Rawling had wiped the blood off Dad's pale face. "Nothing worse. Really. We probably don't even have to mention this to your mother."

Dad woke up 10 minutes after Rawling and I had helped Dad out of his space suit within the safety of the platform buggy's mini-dome. Rawling revived Dad with smelling salts from the first-aid kit.

Several hours passed while Dad recovered. And during that time, the three of us watched the digital video scans, over and over.

Now Rawling was at the controls of the platform buggy, driving us back in the direction of the main dome.

Dad and I sat facing the monitor. With the remote in his hand, Dad again clicked the digital video scan replay, and images flickered onto the screen. I saw on the monitor everything that the robot body had relayed up to the computer on the platform buggy.

The camera surveyed the first alien bodies up and down, slowly. It did the same with the other bodies in the other black boxes. Then the background blurred during the section where I'd raced back to the first bodies, which then began to melt.

Dad clicked the slow-motion button. "It's as if some kind of chemical reaction is taking place. Like the bodies were sealed until we opened the boxes."

"And then," Rawling added as he continued to drive, "the carbon dioxide of Mars's atmosphere must have re-acted with a substance on the clear coating, turning it into an acid. . . . Hold on. I have to talk to Steven." Rawling called up the main dome on our field radio.

While Rawling was patched in to Steven, I kept my eyes on the monitor, only half listening to Rawling's report.

"We'll relay all the video images immediately," Rawling said to Blaine Steven. "It appears the artifacts had some sort of self-destruct timer. Everything was destroyed, but we've got it all on video."

On the monitor, the first box exploded outward.

"Can you back up a few frames and go to super slow motion?" I asked Dad.

As Dad clicked back a few frames, Rawling continued to drive and speak into the field radio at the front of the platform.

"Please confirm by calling back when you receive the satellite relay," Rawling told Blaine Steven. "I don't want to imagine the worst, but if anything should happen to us on the way back to the dome, I'd want to know that copies of the video footage are safe with you. What we saw down there was absolutely incredible. This can't be lost to the rest of humankind."

Again, I was barely listening to Rawling. I was watching hard for the source of the explosion.

Because the digital video scan was advancing frame by frame, I was able to see the first bloom of bright light in the bottom rear of the black box, in the first instant of the explosion.

"Stop," I asked Dad. "Back it up again. Two frames. Then hold."

"Yes," Rawling was saying. "Unfortunately, there's no other evidence but the video feed. Once you have it, you've got all that we've got. But it should be enough to convince the Science Agency committee that something incredible is here. Somehow those aliens had the technology for antigravity and perpetual motion."

I wasn't sure if I saw on the monitor what my mind thought I saw.

"We'll be back as soon as possible," Rawling said. "See you then."

"Stop!" I shouted, suddenly afraid.

Rawling hung up the radio speaker.

"But I've got it stopped," Dad said to me. The frame was frozen on the monitor.

"No," I said. "Stop the platform buggy! Now!"

There, on the monitor, in the back corner of one of the black boxes, was a small, gray, plastic box with antennas. If I was right, that little gray box on the monitor had triggered the explosion that began in the next frame.

And, if I was right, that small, gray, plastic box was just like the one I'd seen on the axle of the platform buggy when I fixed the tire.

CHAPTER 21

Whoever this is, you are mean and nasty and rotten to pretend you are Tyce Sanders. Respect the memory of his death. Get off his computer and leave it alone. He was a true space hero. And he was my friend. I miss him very much. Please do not send me another E-mail.

I stared at the screen of the mainframe computer on the platform buggy.

We were parked about five miles from the dome, behind a range of short mountains. It was the middle of the day, and I'd sent Ashley an E-mail on this computer about 10 minutes earlier.

I grinned at Ashley's return message. I could picture her and her mad frown as she banged at her keyboard. I was glad to read that she liked me.

I hit the reply button on her E-mail. All the dome's computers were set up with an Internet system that let scientists and tekkies send each other electronic messages.

The reply box appeared on my computer screen.

Ashley. It really is me. I know that everyone under the dome

thinks we are dead. And my guess is that Blaine Steven an-
nounced it, right? But we're alive. It's important you keep this
a secret. Please e-mail me back and tell me that you will help.

I stared at the computer screen.

Rawling and Dad were snoozing on the platform beds
behind me. Taking turns, they had driven all of the previous
night and the beginning of this day to get here.

But our mission wasn't finished.

We couldn't let anyone at the dome see the platform
buggy. We guessed by now that they all believed it had
been blown up in a mysterious accident. Dad was upset
thinking how sad and upset Mom must be. He wanted to
get back to the dome as soon as possible to let her know
we were alive. The thought of how Mom must be feeling
tore me up inside, too.

But we had to wait. On the long drive back, Dad and
Rawling had begun to guess what had happened. If they
were right, we'd find out soon.

But only with Ashley's help.

The computer gave a little chirp, telling me that an
E-mail had arrived.

If you don't stop with these messages, I'll go straight to the
director. He'll track the message to see where it came from.
I'll make sure you're punished. How could you dare pretend
to be Tyce? Don't send me any more messages . . . please.

I knew by now that Mom would be crying. Dad and I
wanted to send an E-mail to her, but Rawling asked us to
wait just a few hours. Rawling was afraid that if Mom
showed happiness or excitement, then Director Blaine Steven might wonder what was happening.

And it was Blaine Steven who we needed to get. By himself. Away from the dome.

But how could I convince Ashley to help us? How could I convince her I was alive? That the E-mail messages truly were coming from me?

I remembered something.

I reached into my pocket and held it in my hand.

Ashley, you gave me one of your silver earrings. Remember? The cross. You said it helped you not to be afraid of anything because it reminded you of Jesus and heaven. No one else would know about that except for me, right? Every night, when I said my prayers, I thought of the cross. And I thought of you. I prayed for you like I hope you were praying for me.

I hit the send button.

Snores reached me. What was it about adults that made them snore? And what about those hairs on their shoulders and the backs of their arms? And the nostril hairs? And . . .

Thirty seconds later, her reply came.

Tyce? I want so badly to believe it's you. But maybe the real Tyce told someone about the cross before leaving the dome. And maybe you heard about it and are pretending to be him, which would be the meanest thing in the world to do. So if you are Tyce Sanders, tell me what question I asked you on the day you left the dome.

I grinned. How could I forget her question? It was something to think about whenever I could, especially after what Dad and I had talked about.

I began to keyboard a reply.

Why is there something instead of nothing? Why not nothing? And where did the something come from? Did it exist forever? But how can something exist forever? But if first there was nothing, how did the nothing suddenly become something? How can stars and planets just come from empty air? Did time exist before the universe started? If time didn't exist, what was happening before time began?

Once again, I sent the message.

I leaned back in my wheelchair and waited.

The snoring behind me grew louder as Dad and Rawling fell deeper and deeper into sleep.

The computer chirped.

I scanned her message.

Tyce, it is you! What happened? I mean, at the dome Director Steven announced that the platform buggy had exploded. He said there was no g.p.u. signal, so you weren't traceable. The satellite photos showed a small crater where the platform buggy had sent its last signal. But if it didn't explode, why have you guys let everyone at the dome think you are dead?

I leaned forward in my wheelchair. Rawling had jotted down on a piece of paper the instructions to give to Ashley.

I decided to dash off a quick E-mail to her before I began to keyboard them in.

Ashley, don't let anyone know we are alive. Tonight they'll find out anyway, and then I can explain. But first you need to help us. At eight o'clock tonight, go to the dome entrance. Let me in without anyone knowing it. In the meantime, I'll be sending another long E-mail with more instructions.

Again, I sent the message.

I thought about our plan.

The dome entrance had two ways of getting in. The first, of course, was through the large doors that allowed platform buggies in and out of the dome. The second was a normal-sized door so that tekkies and scientists could just walk out in space suits.

Tyce, I'll keep it a secret. (So will Flip and Flop! They're sitting right beside me.) And I'll meet you there at eight o'clock. I think I know a way to get you in secretly. See you then.

Your happy, happy friend, Ashley

I sighed with satisfaction. Dad and Rawling would be happy to hear it too. If the rest of our plan worked, it would be great. If not . . .

I didn't want to think about it.

Actually, it was tough to think about anything.

Not with how both of them snored.

I tore a little strip of paper off the note Rawling had written.

I wheeled over to where Dad was asleep and snoring like a chainsaw.

I tickled the inside of his nostril with the paper.

Asleep, he swatted at it.

I tickled more.

He snorted and grunted and finally hit himself in the nose so hard that it woke him up.

"Hi," I said innocently. "Want to hear about Ashley?"

CHAPTER 22

"What nonsense is this? Calling me here this late at night?"

The angry hiss belonged to Director Blaine Steven. He directed his questions to Ashley, who sat quietly on a bench near the tall, thick plants in the center of the dome, where she and I had met just an hour earlier.

"Thank you for coming," she said sweetly.

It was dim. This late—just before nine o'clock—the dome lights were turned down. Most scientists and tekkies were reading or at their personal computers or getting ready to sleep. At the dome, the policy was early to bed and early to rise.

"I wouldn't be here if you hadn't sent that crazy message," Director Steven continued in his low growl. Steven, who was over 60, ran his hands through his thick, wavy gray hair as he talked. "What do you mean, Tyce Sanders sent you a message?"

"The aliens are fake," Ashley said bluntly. Director Steven stood in front of her, arms crossed, as Ashley continued. "When an asteroid hit nearby, causing a quake, someone here triggered a bomb that exposed the black

97

boxes. Just so people would think it was the asteroid that uncovered them. But all along, the so-called aliens had been set up and waiting. The Science Agency had been tracking the asteroid and knew when it would hit."

"What?!"

"It's in the E-mail Tyce sent me."

That was true. Rawling and Dad had come up with the theory, hoping it had enough truth in it to be able to bluff Steven into admitting more. I'd sent it to Ashley by E-mail so she could be ready for this meeting.

"That's the most outrageous thing I've heard. Tyce is a space hero. I know you miss him badly, but you shouldn't make things up."

"You see," Ashley continued calmly, "when the dome was first established over 14 years ago, those black boxes were buried by someone on a secret mission from the dome. They were left there for an emergency."

"I've had enough out of you." Director Steven tried to look angry, but he couldn't quite pull it off. He seemed worried, and he looked around a few times as though he wondered if anyone was overhearing this.

"It was planned for the day or two before people on Earth who were part of the United Nations would have to decide whether or not to continue funding the dome. Fake aliens and fake antigravity and fake perpetual motion. If people believed in it, they wouldn't care how much was spent to keep the Project going."

"All of this is in your E-mail?"

It was. Rawling and Dad had had a lot of time to think this through—ever since the explosion that was supposed to kill us. Those boxes were set up to *look* very convincing. But if the stuff inside could have been examined, it could easily have been seen as fake. We were convinced that was the reason everything was rigged to blow up.

The revolving globe? We'd guessed that, with electromagnetics from an energy source hidden underneath the box, triggered by the opening of the door, a globe would float, repelled by magnetics. Which was why the robot had short-circuited once the arm reached inside and touched the invisible currents.

"And more," Ashley said, plunging ahead and playing her role perfectly. "Tyce wrote that once the digital video scan had been made, someone here at the dome triggered devices to destroy all the alien artifacts. Because if anyone examined the aliens or the antigravity device, everybody would know they were fakes. But if video was all that remained, no one could dispute it."

"Someone at the dome?" he asked, worry in his voice.

Someone, I thought, *who at first insisted on reports every six hours but then kept contacting us every hour. Someone who had been speaking to Rawling on the radio while Dad and I were down at the black boxes, showing Rawling the aliens on the monitor. Someone who had heard all about it from Rawling as it happened. Someone who waited until the video feed had been beamed back to the dome by satellite and then . . .*

"Yes," Ashley told Director Steven. Her face was concerned. "Someone who then triggered a bomb to destroy the platform buggy. That explosion wasn't an accident. It was on purpose. Someone here at the dome wanted to kill the only witnesses to the fake aliens. With them dead, only the video would remain. People on Earth would fund the dome for another hundred years, hoping to find the secrets behind antigravity or perpetual motion. Secrets that don't exist."

Director Steven now ran his hands wildly through his hair. He glanced in all directions, then gave Ashley his attention.

"And you have all this on E-mail? From Tyce? He sent it before the explosion?"

"It's on my computer," Ashley said, ignoring the question about the explosion.

"Has anyone else seen it?"

"No," she said. "I thought I should let you be the first to know."

"No one else has seen it."

"I just told you that."

"I needed to be sure," Director Steven said. "Thank you."

"You're welcome. Are you going to find out who triggered the devices? Are you going to tell people the aliens were fakes, planted by an Earth mission?"

"Let's go for a walk," Director Steven answered.

"Walk?"

With a sudden movement, he grabbed Ashley's wrist and pulled her to her feet. Then he tightened his arm around her waist and clapped a hand over her mouth so she couldn't scream.

"A long walk," he said in a menacing tone. "Out on the surface of the planet."

CHAPTER 23

I'd been waiting for this moment.

In the robot body, I rolled out from behind the plants that had kept me hidden from Director Steven. With his back to me and one arm wrapped around Ashley's waist, he didn't see me coming. So I reached out and grabbed his wrist with titanium fingers. I locked my grip.

"Let her go," I demanded.

Director Steven found himself looking straight into my front video lens. His eyes bulged with surprise. Not at my appearance, though that would have surprised most people.

No, Director Steven knew what the robot body looked like. That's not what surprised him.

"Impossible," he said. He had to know as soon as he saw the robot body that we hadn't been blown up.

"Not impossible. Dad and Rawling are in the platform buggy, about five miles from here, where they are letting me control this robot body. Now let her go."

I tightened my grip. The titanium fingers of the robot body were capable of bending bars of steel. He screamed in pain. I lessened the grip slightly, but did not release his arm.

"Let her go."

Reluctantly, he did.

"It was you," I said. "Someone high up in the Science Agency on Earth is in on it too, right? So you were placed back as director?"

"This is insane," he protested.

Ashley backed away from Director Steven. Her face was not afraid but angry. "Jerk!" she said to him. She kicked him in the shins, then sat down on the bench.

"It is not insane," I said. I held out my other hand. "Recognize this?"

Director Steven drew in a big breath of surprise. He tried to pull himself out of my grip.

"So you do recognize it," I said.

I held a small, gray, plastic box, with what looked like antennas sticking out of the sides. It was the same box we'd pulled off the axle of the platform buggy. Filled with high-powered explosive devices, it was just like the one on the video that had exploded the black boxes.

"Take it outside," Director Steven said, his eyes wide as he stared at it in my hand.

"Outside? Why?"

After I'd seen the small, gray, plastic box on the monitor and remembered the one on the axle, Dad and Rawling had gone out of the platform buggy to remove the box. They'd taken the cover off but left the explosives intact, with the antennas in place. We'd driven safely away, leaving the explosives near the base of a hill. It hadn't surprised us when it blew only 15 minutes later, taking much of the hillside with it, leaving people at the dome with the mistaken impression that we'd died. And that's when Rawling and Dad had come up with their theory.

"Just take it outside!" Director Steven was frantic. "The whole dome could be destroyed!"

But a theory was only a theory unless it could be proved. Rawling had reassembled the cover of the gray box and inserted wires that would look like antennas. But only in dim lighting. Like right here and right now.

"Destroyed?" I said. "Are you suggesting this thing in my hand is a bomb? But how could you know, unless you were the person behind this?"

"No! No!" Director Steven finally realized what he might have admitted.

"Well," I said, "if it is *not* a bomb, we have nothing to worry about. Why not go for a ride in the other platform buggy? Just you and me. Once outside the dome, we will see if it is an explosive or not. How does that sound?"

"No!"

If the bomb went off, Director Steven realized he'd be the only one hurt. I, after all, was controlling the robot body. If it was destroyed, it wouldn't harm me.

"No? You do not want to go for a ride? Because maybe you know what this is?"

"Yes," he said. "I do. Let go of me, and I'll tell you everything."

I let go of his arm.

He backed away from me. He grinned.

"I'm going to go get security," he said. "They'll take you away. And Ashley. When I erase her computer files, it will be your word against mine."

"The explosive," I said.

"I doubt very much you'll do anything with it here. In the

dome? Where it will kill Ashley and your mother and everyone else?"

Another grin of victory.

"Fool," he said.

He turned and ran before I could stop him.

I rolled my robot body around to face Ashley.

She was frowning.

"That didn't work exactly like you planned," she said.

"Are you kidding?" I pointed at my video lens. "From the moment he got here, I recorded every word."

EPILOGUE

08.06.2039

   I don t really want to be sitting here in front of
my computer. It s early evening, and I want to leave
my mini-dome and go up to the telescope. But I
know I d better put the rest of what happened into
my diary while it s still fresh in my head.

   Rawling and Dad had guessed right. That s why
we d taken so many hours to return to the dome.
They d spent a lot of time throwing ideas back and
forth until they d realized exactly why and how all
of it must have happened.

   The entire alien thing was fake. It had been set
up secretly right when the dome was first established. Director Steven, of course, had been part of
it from the beginning. All those years ago Science
Agency tekkies on Earth had made those fakes.
And just to show how coldly careful the Science
Agency had been, they d used two tekkies who
were battling terminal cancer, knowing that when
they died they d take their secret with them. The
Agency had even planned the alien discovery by

projecting which asteroid would hit 15 years later, because even back then the science committee knew the Mars Project funding would come up for review around that time.

Why go to so much effort for something fake?

How about $200 billion a year? That s what the Mars Project needs. And that s what it was going to get for another 10 years when the videos arrived at the United Nations budget committee by digital satellite . . . just in the nick of time to get everybody excited about aliens and new technology. Let s see . . . that s a total of $2 trillion. Not bad for a fake setup. And a couple of murders, if it had worked.

Director Blaine Steven had . . .

I stopped keyboarding as a familiar chime on my computer alerted me to a new E-mail message. I saved my diary writing but didn't close the program.

I clicked on my E-mail alert.

Tyce, are you going to meet me tonight? I want to talk.

I smiled and sent Ashley a message.

Talk? How about up at the telescope?

Seconds later, she wrote back.

Sounds good. How about I stop by and we'll go together? I'll bring Flip and Flop. They've been restless. I think they miss you!

I smiled again.

Come on over. And yes, bring the koalas. I miss them too.

I sent the message, then returned to my diary.

Director Steven had heard about our planned trip from one of his tekkie moles someone who spied for him and kept him informed of things happening at the dome. It was a tekkie whose job was to help prepare the platform buggies for field trips. This tekkie had planted the bomb.

And after we left the dome, this same tekkie had helped ex-Director Steven send a coded message to the higher-ups in the Science Agency who had helped him set up this plan many years ago, while Steven was still on Earth. They pulled the strings to get Steven put in place as dome director again. From there, all that Director Steven needed to do was monitor our progress. As soon as he received the digital video scans, it served his purposes to get rid of the only witnesses to the fake aliens.

But now Steven is back under guard, along with the tekkie who helped him. They ll be going back to Earth on the next shuttle to face criminal charges there.

As for the funding, the funny part is this: it went through, without the alien report. Members of the budget committee didn t even hear about the aliens. With a 7 5 vote in favor of budgeting more money, they decided to keep the dome going simply because it truly was important to Earth. Although Steven had sent the digital video scans back to Earth by satellite transmission, Dad and Rawling followed them up with the whole report about fakes. The Science Agency kept all of this out of the public news and is now investigating who on Earth was involved.

Yet without a flat tire, it would have turned out much differently. I shiver when I think of what would have happened to Dad and Rawling and me out on the surface of Mars if I hadn't seen that small gray box.

But all thoughts about death are scary. I can understand why people would rather listen to music or watch television or play computer games or do anything else to distract themselves from wondering about death. Because then you have to ask questions about God and why we're here and how the universe started and . . .

I stopped keyboarding again. And smiled again. Tonight I'd be happy to talk about all of this with Ashley. It was great having a friend my age.

I heard her voice as she called out for me and then Mom's voice as she told Ashley I was in my room.

I saved my writing, shut down my computer, and turned my wheelchair around so that I was facing her when she walked into my room.

"Hey," I said. "You got here fast."

"I ran," she said. "I've got some news. You've got to promise to keep it secret. At least until my father announces it officially."

"Sure."

She stepped closer and spoke in a whisper. "Interested in going to Jupiter?"

CAN WE EXPECT SCIENCE TO BE OUR SAVIOR?

For the first ten thousand years of recorded human history, the fastest that any human could travel was the speed of a galloping horse. (Unless someone wanted to jump off a building or a cliff!) Horse-drawn wagons were very slow, wind-powered ships were slow, the first trains were slow, and even the first automobiles were slow.

It's only in the last hundred years or so—the tiniest sliver of time—that technology has allowed us to travel faster. Some cars go as fast as two hundred miles an hour. Airplanes can go faster than sound. A journey that took the early American settlers weeks or months by wagon over dangerous territory, we can accomplish in hours on an interstate in air-conditioned comfort.

In fact, thanks to science and technology, most of us truly live better than kings did only one hundred years ago. We live in heated homes with running water, televisions, and washers and dryers. Doctors no longer try to cure us by applying leeches to our heads to suck blood; we can get the best of modern drugs and operations. We're protected by electronic security systems and police forces; we probably don't lie awake at night worrying about barbarians tearing down our town. We store our wealth in electronic binary codes in bank computers, not in piles of gold or silver that armies can steal.

And these improvements in science and technology are happening faster and faster. After all, it was only a little more than 30 years ago that a man first stepped on the moon.

Now sport utility vehicles have more technology than the first spaceships, and your desktop computer has more calculating power than the computers that placed the first men on the moon. With cell phones and computers, you can instantly communicate through satellites to locations anywhere in the world.

Medicine? Your body can be vaccinated, wired, and soon, cloned.

Even color televisions were first invented only 40 years ago. Now you can entertain yourself with the virtual reality of music videos, computer games, and theater screens three stories tall.

Science and technology are staggering, amazing, incredible. Who knows how many more leaps ahead we will be by A.D. 2039, the date of this story? And what's even more exciting is that *you,* like Tyce Sanders and his virtual-reality missions, may be the one who helps discover this new technology!

But in all the excitement, don't forget to ask the most important questions about life, science, and faith. Can science and technology stop crime? Can they prevent heartache, loneliness, fear? Can they make families perfect? Can they prevent death?

The answer to all of the questions is obvious.

No.

Although the conditions around you have improved with blinding speed, you can still suffer pain, guilt, heartache, fear, and loneliness deep inside you. Where it matters.

Those who look to science and technology to save us as a human race assume we just don't know enough yet. But learning more about our world and how it works doesn't make problems go away. The answer is all too obvious. All you need to do is read the headlines of a newspaper or watch the daily news to see it.

The real problem—sadly—is the choices we make. Some are good choices. Others are hurtful, evil choices. Because God loves us, he gives us the power to choose. But then we have to live with the consequences.

The bottom line is that science and technology are incredible tools for exploring what it means to be human— and for helping other humans, if used properly. But science and technology cannot change anyone's heart. And they'll never give meaning or hope or peace to your life.

Instead of looking to science for solutions, look to the God of the Bible. After all, he's the one who created you, who knows you inside and out, and wants the best for you. He's the only one who can change your heart. He's the only true Savior of all humankind.

ABOUT THE AUTHOR

Sigmund Brouwer and his wife, recording artist Cindy Morgan, split living between Red Deer, Alberta, Canada, and Nashville, Tennessee. He has written several series of juvenile fiction and eight novels. Sigmund loves sports and plays golf and hockey. He also enjoys visiting schools to talk about books. He welcomes visitors to his Web site at www.coolreading.com, where he and a bunch of other authors like to hang out in cyberspace.

mars
DIARIES
are you ready?

Set in an experimental community on Mars in the years 2039–2043, the Mars Diaries feature teen virtual-reality specialist Tyce Sanders. Life on the red planet is not always easy, but it is definitely exciting. As Tyce explores his strange surroundings, he also finds that the mysteries of the planet point to his greatest discovery—a new relationship with God.

MISSION 1: Oxygen Level Zero
Time was running out....

MISSION 2: Alien Pursuit
"Help me!" And the radio went dead....

MISSION 3: Time Bomb
A quake rocks the red planet, uncovering a long-kept secret....

MISSION 4: Hammerhead
I was dead center in the laser target controls....

MISSION 5: Sole Survivor
Scientists buried alive at cave-in site!

MISSION 6: Moon Racer
Everyone has a motive...and secrets. The truth must be found before it's too late.

MISSION 7: Countdown
20 soldiers, 20 neuron rifles. There was nowhere to run. Nowhere to hide....

MISSION 8: Robot War
Ashley and I are their only hope, and they think we're traitors.

MISSION 9: Manchurian Sector
I was in trouble...and I couldn't trust anyone.

MISSION 10: Last Stand
Invasion was imminent ... and we'd lost all contact with Earth.

Visit Tyce on-line!

- O Learn more about the red planet from a real expert
- O Great contests and awesome prizes
- O Fun quizzes and games
- O Find out when the next book is coming out

mars DIARIES

Discover the latest news about the Mars Diaries.
Visit www.marsdiaries.com